What people are saying about

# Kill All Normies

Amidst the chaos of our times, it is a relief to have a brilliant and fearless critic like Angela Nagle to turn to. Unwilling to stomach the liberal shibboleths that fail to adequately explain the emergence and significance of right-wing subculture, she's the only one willing to descend into the grimiest of Internet grottos and give us the benefit of her incisive and cool-headed analysis. (And thank god too, because I'm sure as hell not doing it.)
**Amber A'Lee Frost**, Chapo Trap House

Angela Nagle is one of the few writers anywhere who has consistently refused to hold a double standard for virulent racism and misogyny even when it came in edgy countercultural packaging. Kill All Normies is a brilliant exposé of the new faces of online nihilism and fascism, which can no longer be explained away as doing it "for the lulz".
**David Golumbia**, Author of *The Politics of Bitcoin: Software as Right-Wing Extremism*

With a liberal left dangerously lost in the stormy waters of middle class self-flagellation, Angela Nagle is the lighthouse keeper showing us the way out. Her writing is unsparing in its diagnosis but never cruel. Unlike much of the Left who've grown far too accustomed to marginalization and defeat, Nagle still believes in politics as the only way of changing an increasingly brutal world. She is the writer and social critic I've been waiting for.
**Connor Kilpatrick**, *Jacobin* magazine

# Kill All
# Normies

# Kill All Normies

The online culture wars from Tumblr and
4chan to the alt-right and Trump

Angela Nagle

Winchester, UK
Washington, USA

First published by Zero Books, 2017
Zero Books is an imprint of John Hunt Publishing Ltd., Laurel House, Station Approach,
Alresford, Hants, SO24 9JH, UK
office1@jhpbooks.net
www.johnhuntpublishing.com
www.zero-books.net

For distributor details and how to order please visit the 'Ordering' section on our website.

Text copyright: Angela Nagle 2017

ISBN: 978 1 78535 543 1
978 1 78535 544 8 (ebook)
Library of Congress Control Number: 2017934035

A CIP catalogue record for this book is available from the British Library.

Design: Stuart Davies


Printed and bound by CPI Group (UK) Ltd, Croydon, CR0 4YY, UK

We operate a distinctive and ethical publishing philosophy in
all areas of our business, from our global network of authors to
production and worldwide distribution.

# Contents

# Introduction

# From Hope to Harambe

In the lead-up to the election of Barack Obama in 2008, his message of hope was publicly and with great earnestness shared by vast numbers of liberals online, eager to show their love for the first black president, ecstatic to be part of what felt like a positive mass-cultural moment. After George W. Bush, who had waged wars in Iraq and Afghanistan, and embarrassed educated people with his Southern style, and his regular gaffs and grammatical mistakes or 'Bushisms', the feeling of shame among US liberals was captured at the time by books like Michael Moore's *Stupid White Men*.

In stark contrast Obama was articulate, sophisticated, erudite and cosmopolitan. In the media spectacle of his election Oprah cried, Beyoncé sang and crowds of young, adoring fans rejoiced. Even some of the icy hearts of those significantly to the left of the Democratic Party were temporarily melted in what felt like a mass outpouring of positivity and hope, an egalitarian dream realized.

Hillary Clinton tried to repeat this formula in 2016 by dancing on *The Ellen DeGeneres Show*, drafting in Beyoncé once again, assuring listeners of her penchant for hot sauce and attracting feminist celebrities like Lena Dunham with the 'I'm With Her' slogan. However, instead, she became a source of comedy and ridicule among large online audiences from right across the political spectrum. When she solemnly condemned a new Internet age right-wing movement as part of Trump's 'basket of deplorables', the massed online ranks of the target of her comments collectively erupted in memes, mockery and celebration.

How did we get from those earnest hopeful days broadcast across the media mainstream to where we are now? This book covers this period from the perspective of Internet-culture and subcultures, tracing the online culture wars that have raged on below the line and below the radar of mainstream media throughout the period over feminism, sexuality, gender identity, racism, free speech and political correctness. This was unlike the culture wars of the 60s or the 90s, in which a typically older age cohort of moral and cultural conservatives fought against a tide of cultural secularization and liberalism among the young. This online backlash was able to mobilize a strange vanguard of teenage gamers, pseudonymous swastika-posting anime lovers, ironic *South Park* conservatives, anti-feminist pranksters, nerdish harassers and meme-making trolls whose dark humor and love of transgression for its own sake made it hard to know what political views were genuinely held and what were merely, as they used to say, for the lulz. What seemed to hold them all together in their obscurity was a love of mocking the earnestness and moral self-flattery of what felt like a tired liberal intellectual conformity running right through from establishment liberal politics to the more militant enforcers of new sensitivities from the wackiest corners of Tumblr to campus politics.

Through this period we can also see the death of what remained of a mass culture sensibility, in which there was still a mainstream media arena and a mainstream sense of culture and the public. The triumph of the Trumpians was also a win in the war against this mainstream media, which is now held in contempt by many average voters and the weird irony-laden Internet subcultures from right and left, who equally set themselves apart from this hated mainstream. It is a career disaster now to signal your left-behind cluelessness as a basic bitch, a normie or a member of the corrupt media mainstream in any way. Instead, we see online the emergence of a new kind of anti-establishment sensibility expressing itself in the kind of DIY culture of memes and user-generated content that cyberutopian true believers have evangelized about for many years but had not imagined taking on this particular political form.

Compare the first election won by Obama, in which social media devotees reproduced the iconic but official blue-and-red stylized stencil portrait of the new president with HOPE printed across the bottom, a portrait created by artist Shepard Fairey and approved by the official Obama campaign, to the bursting forth of irreverent mainstream-baffling meme culture during the last race, in which the Bernie Sanders Dank Meme Stash Facebook page and The Donald subreddit defined the tone of the race for a young and newly politicized generation, with the mainstream media desperately trying to catch up with a subcultural in-joke style to suit two emergent anti-establishment waves of the right and left. Writers like Manuel Castells and numerous commentators in the *Wired* magazine milieu told us of the coming of a networked society, in which old hierarchical models of business and culture would be replaced by the wisdom of crowds, the swarm, the hive mind, citizen journalism and user-generated content. They got their wish, but it's not quite the utopian vision they were hoping for.

As old media dies, gatekeepers of cultural sensibilities and etiquette have been overthrown, notions of popular taste maintained by a small creative class are now perpetually outpaced by viral online content from obscure sources, and culture industry consumers have been replaced by constantly online, instant content producers. The year 2016 may be remembered as the year the media mainstream's hold over formal politics died. A thousand Trump Pepe memes bloomed and a strongman larger-than-life Twitter troll who showed open hostility to the mainstream media and to both party establishments took The White House without them.

One of the early significant moments of rupture in mainstream Internet-culture sensibilities was the viral Kony 2012 video. You can map a trajectory through the dominant styles from virtue to cynical inscrutable irony, roughly from *Kony 2012* to the Harambe meme explosion in 2016. The *Kony 2012* film's purpose was to promote the charity campaign Stop Kony, which itself aimed to have the Ugandan militia leader Joseph Kony arrested by the end of 2012. The film received over 100 million views and went so viral that one poll suggested half of young adult Americans heard about it in the days following the video's release, causing its website to crash. *TIME* magazine called it the most viral video ever made. On Facebook and Twitter, a vast audience of Western young people normally pretty indifferent to the activities of Ugandan war criminals shared the video, with urgent emotional exclamations attached, which we might now cynically call 'virtue signaling'.

But then the video and the campaign started to come under criticism from Ugandans, experts on the region, and even their Head of State. Denunciations of the video began to pour in for its crass oversimplification, inaccuracy, emotional manipulation and 'slacktivism' – a now common pejorative also called 'clicktivism'. A mass screening of the film in Uganda was met with jeering and hostility, as viewers were angered that the film was focused on the US filmmaker, while neglecting Kony's victims. Western critics eager for shares of righteous approval rushed to expose the insufficient virtue of *Kony 2012* and its mainstream supporters.

Then, still at the height of the video's viral fame, Jason Russell, the filmmaker, was arrested and detained for psychiatric evaluation after his public breakdown was filmed and released online. This became yet another viral video in which he could be seen outdoors naked and shouting, hitting the ground, masturbating and vandalizing cars.

At a dizzying pace, the Kony story had run a now familiar course from mainstream virtue to competitive virtue hot takes to disgrace to *Schadenfreude*, which would become a standard plot of dark online spectacles in the years that followed. Many of those who had shared the video in the spirit of global goodwill were sheepishly taking it down. Earnest, feel-good, easily shared concern had been replaced in a matter of days with the darkest side of the return of a more native, pre-monetized, anonymous Internet-culture – *Schadenfreude*, deep cynicism and the now unstoppable force of public humiliation as viral entertainment.

By 2016, after countless repeats of the *Kony 2012* cycle from virtue to disgrace, a spirit of deep nihilistic cynicism and reactive irony bubbled up to the surface of mainstream Internet-culture and an absurd in-jokey forum humor became dominant. When a gorilla named Harambe was shot dead at the Cincinnati Zoo that year after a child fell into his enclosure, the usual cycles of public displays of outrage online began as expected with inevitable competitive virtue signaling. At first, emotional and outraged people online blamed the child's parents for the gorilla's death, with some even petitioning to have the parents prosecuted for their neglect. But then a kind of giddy ironic mocking of the social media spectacle started to take over. The Harambe meme soon became the perfect parody of the sentimentality and absurd priorities of Western liberal performative politics and the online mass hysteria that often characterized it.

On the same day that a post about the incident reached the front page of Reddit news, a petition titled 'Justice for Harambe' was created on Change.org, which called for authorities to hold the child's parents responsible for Harambe's death, gaining hundreds of thousands of signatures. Soon, the mostly ironically used hashtags #JusticeForHarambe and #RIPHarambe began circulating. Song parodies with Harambe inserted into the lyrics were created, and the call to arms 'Dicks Out For Harambe' was quickly turned into a popular expression by comedian Brandon Wardell.

Harambe began appearing in tongue-in-cheek sentimental portraits of beloved celebrities who had died in 2016, like David

Bowie and Prince. One US high school student in a gorilla costume was filmed running along the sidelines at his school's first football game of the season, dragging another student behind him like the little boy in the enclosure before Harambe was shot. The Zoo pleaded with the meme-makers to stop using Harambe hashtags, and bombarding them with tweets and messages. The memes spread to mainstream media, when a young man holding a 'Bush Did Harambe' sign, a reference also to the 9/11 'truther' conspiracy, appeared on MSNBC live outside the Democratic National Convention.

Matt Christman from the podcast Chapo Trap House, itself a knowing product of contemporary irony-saturated online culture, unsentimentally but accurately summed it up saying: 'the popularity of Harambe jokes proves that people want to laugh about murder but feel bad about it.' Christman also noted on one podcast that Harambe mania really took off after the Orlando nightclub massacre in a gay club, carried out by a shooter pledging allegiance to ISIS.

Responding to highly mediated tragedies with insensitive pranking and irony had been a staple of online trolling cultures for many years before, but Harambe was the first case attracting such large numbers of people online wanting to get in on the in-joke. It went viral too, because it hit at a time when a particular style of humorless, self-righteous, right-on social media sentimentality had already reached such an absurd peak that the once obscure style of ironic cynical mockery also emerged into more mainstream Internet-culture as a counterforce.

Although it worked as a brilliantly absurd parody, and was embraced by ironists from left to right, what came to complicate the detached humor is that, as in so many other similar cases, it also allowed cover for genuinely sinister things to hide amid the maze of irony. For example, Harambe was referenced by harassers in the hate campaign led against *Ghostbusters* star Leslie Jones, with largely anonymous threats and comparisons of her to the gorilla. This barrage of abuse came her way after Milo Yiannopoulos, the English gay conservative turned alt-light celebrity, tweeted a series of insults at her and said, among other things, that she looked like 'a black dude'. The harassment campaign against her for finding herself in Milo's firing line led to, among other things, her website being hacked and nude photos of her being circulated online.

Given the Harambe meme became a favorite of alt-right abusers, was it then just old-fashioned racism dressed up as Internet-savvy satire, as it appealed most to those seeking to mock liberal sensitivities? Or was it a clever parody of the inane hysteria and faux-politics of liberal Internet-culture? Do those involved in such memes any longer know what motivated them and if they themselves are being ironic or not? Is it possible that they are both ironic parodists and earnest actors in a media phenomenon at the same time?

A hacker who goes by the Twitter handle @prom hacked into the account of Cincinnati Zoo director Thane Maynard tweeting #DicksOutForHarambe from his account. When asked about his motivations, though, he told the *New York Daily News* he was 'not sure' why he hacked Maynard's account, saying: 'At the time when it actually happened I was kinda angry at the dude who shot him.'

It was amid this ironical in-jokey maze of meaning that the online culture wars played out, that Trump got elected and that what we now call the alt-right came to prominence. Every bizarre event, new identity and strange subcultural behavior that baffles general audiences when they eventually make the mainstream media, from otherkin to far right Pepe memes, can be understood as a response to a response to a response, each one responding angrily to the existence of the other. Trumpian meme-makers ramped up their taboo-breaking anti-PC style in response to gender-bending Tumblr users, who themselves then became more sensitive, more convinced of the racism, misogyny and hetero-normative oppression of the world outside of their online subcultures. At the same time, the 'deplorables', from the Trumpian trolls to the alt-right, view the Hillary loyalists – the entrenched identity politics of Tumblr and the intersectional anti-free speech campus left – as evidence of their equally bleak view of a rapidly declining Western civilization, as both sides have become increasingly unmoored to any cultural mainstream, which scarcely resembles either bleak vision.

The once obscure call-out culture of the left emanating from Tumblr-style campus-based identity politics reached its peak during this period, in which everything from eating noodles to reading Shakespeare was declared 'problematic', and even the most mundane acts 'misogynist' and 'white supremacist'. While taboo and anti-moral ideologies festered in the dark corners of the anonymous Internet, the de-anonymized social media platforms, where most young people now develop their political ideas for the first time, became a panopticon, in which the many lived in fear of observation from the eagle eye of an offended organizer of public shaming. At the height of its power, the dreaded call-out, no matter how minor the transgression or how well intentioned the transgressor, could ruin your reputation, your job or your life. The particular incarnations of the online left and right that exist today are undoubtedly a product of this strange period of ultra puritanism. These obscure online political beginnings became formative for a whole generation, and impacted mainstream sensibilities and even language.

The hysterical liberal call-out produced a breeding ground for an online backlash of irreverent mockery and anti-PC, typified by charismatic figures like Milo. But after crying wolf throughout these years, calling everyone from saccharine pop stars to Justin Trudeau a 'white supremacist' and everyone who wasn't With Her a sexist, the real wolf eventually arrived, in the form of the openly white nationalist alt-right who hid among an online army of ironic in-jokey trolls. When this happened, nobody knew who to take literally anymore, including many of those in the middle of this new online far right themselves. The alt-light figures that became celebrities during this period made their careers exposing the absurdities of online identity politics and the culture of lightly thrown claims of misogyny, racism, ableism, fatphobia, transphobia and so on. However, offline, only one side saw their guy take the office of US president and only one side has in their midst faux-ironic *Sieg Heil* saluting, open white segregationists and genuinely hate-filled, occasionally murderous, misogynists and racists.

Before the overtly racist alt-right were widely known, the more mainstream alt-light largely flattered it, gave it glowing write-ups in *Breitbart* and elsewhere, had its spokespeople on their YouTube shows and promoted it on social media. Nevertheless, when Milo's sudden career implosion happened later they didn't return the favor, which I think may be setting a precedent for a future in which the playfully transgressive alt-light unwittingly play the useful idiots for those with much more serious political aims. If this dark, anti-Semitic, race segregationist ideology grows in the coming years, with their vision of the future that would necessitate violence, those who made the right attractive will have to take responsibility for having played their role.

This book is an attempt to map the online culture wars that formed the political sensibilities of a generation, to understand and to keep an account of the online battles that may otherwise be forgotten but have nevertheless shaped culture and ideas in a profound way from tiny obscure subcultural beginnings to mainstream public and political life in recent years. It will place contemporary culture wars in some historical context and attempt to untangle the real from the performance, the material from the abstract and the ironic from the faux-ironic, if such a thing is any longer possible.

## Chapter One

# The leaderless digital counter-revolution

It is worth thinking back now to the early 2010s, when cyberutopianism had its biggest resurgence since the 90s, before the dot-com bubble burst. This time it emerged in response to a series of political events around the world from the Arab Spring to the Occupy movement to new politicized hacker movements. Anonymous, Wikileaks and public-square mass protests in Spain and across the Middle East were getting huge coverage in the news, causing a flurry of opinion and analysis pieces about their profound significance. All of these events were being attributed to the rise of social media and characterized as a new leaderless form of digital revolution. The hyperbole and hubris of the moment should have been enough to make anyone skeptical, but most on the left were swept up in the excitement as images of vast crowds in public squares appeared on social media and then in the mainstream media.

Books, social media and countless gushing columns and blogs celebrated the arrival of what cyberutopians of the early Internet had long prophesized. To pick one typical example of the tone at the time, in Heather Brooke's paean *The Revolution Will be Digitized: Dispatches from the information war* she claimed, 'Technology is breaking down traditional social barriers of status, class, power, wealth and geography, replacing them with an ethos of collaboration and transparency.' *Adbusters*, the Canadian anti-consumerist magazine, published a widely shared article by Manuel Castells called 'The Disgust Becomes a Network' when leaderless encampments, organized online, started to appear in Spain and around the world. He argued that what he had been writing about for most of his career – the networked society – had taken a radical new form. BBC journalist Paul Mason wrote

*Why It's Kicking Off Everywhere*, documenting the revolutionaries in Tahrir Square, the Iranian 'Twitter revolution' and the heavily hashtagged Occupy Wall Street protests that spread around the world.

But this fervor died down in just a few short years. The Egyptian revolution led to something worse – the rule of the Muslim Brotherhood. Islamists ran riot in the streets and stories of rapes in the very public square that had shortly before held so much hope came to light. Soon the military dictatorship swept back into power. The Occupy Wall Street demonstrators remained literally aimless and were eventually forced out of public property by police, camp by camp. By the end of 2013, a public-square style movement took place in Ukraine, which started with many of the same scenes of romanticized people-power in the public square. However this time the leaderless network narrative, which was already starting to look a little less convincing, was left aside because the protests quickly erupted into fascist mob rule.

In many of the events that *were* considered part of the leaderless digital revolution narrative, like Occupy Wall Street and the public-square protests in Spain, in which thousands occupied the Puerta del Sol, the Guy Fawkes mask was adopted as a central symbol. But the online origins of the mask and the politically fungible sensibilities that can be traced back through the mask should have offered a clue that another very different variety of leaderless online movement had potential to brew.

After the election of Trump, everyone wanted to know about a new online right-wing movement whose memetic aesthetics seemed to have infiltrated sites from the popular The Donald subreddit to mainstream Internet-culture. In the lead-up to the election, the most famous common imagery was of Pepe the Frog. The name given by the press to this mix of rightist online phenomena including everything from Milo to 4chan to neo-Nazi sites was the 'alt-right'. In its strictest definition though, as an army of Internet pedants quickly pointed out, the alt-right term was used in its own online circles to include only a new wave of overtly white segregationist and white nationalist movements and subcultures, typified by spokespeople like Richard Spencer, who has called for a US white ethno-state and a pan-national white Empire modeled on some approximation of the Roman Empire. The movement's media also includes Scottish video blogger Millennial Woes, Red Ice, sites like Radix and the long-form and book publishers Counter Currents.

In the broader orbit of the alt-right, made up of often warring and sectarian factions, there is an older generation of white advocates who pre-date the alt-right but who the alt-right reads and draws influence from, like Jared Taylor from the site American Renaissance who refers to himself as a 'race realist' and figures like Kevin B. MacDonald, editor of Occidental Observer, described by the Anti-Defamation League as a primary voice of anti-Semitism for far-right intellectuals. The alt-right is, to varying degrees, preoccupied with IQ, European demographic and civilizational decline, cultural decadence, cultural Marxism, anti-egalitarianism and Islamification but most importantly, as the name suggests, with creating an alternative to the right-wing conservative establishment, who they dismiss as 'cuckservatives' for their soft Christian passivity and for metaphorically cuckholding their womenfolk/nation/race to the non-white foreign invader.

Then there is a range of more obscure rightist anti-egalitarian reactionary tendencies like the earlier neoreaction movement or NRx, which includes thinkers and bloggers like Mencius Moldbug and Nick Land, creators of the influential ideas of 'the Cathedral' and the latter the 'Dark Enlightenment'. The idea of the Cathedral closely resembles Marxian critical theory's understanding of ideology, as an all-encompassing system and prison of the mind. The Dark Enlightenment is an ironic play on the idea of the Enlightenment, based on a suspicion of progress and rejecting the liberal paradigm. Among all alt-right thinkers Land is the greatest misfit, once closer to the radical Accelerationist school of thought and still a highly idiosyncratic thinker, he is not so easily categorized. Within the radical right libertarian pro-tech tendency, common preoccupations include Bitcoin, Seasteading – Peter Theil's idea to create a separate state off the coast of the US – and rightist elite applications of transhumanism.

But of course what we call the alt-right today could never have had any connection to the mainstream and to a new generation of young people if it only came in the form of lengthy treatises on obscure blogs. It was the image- and humor-based culture of the irreverent meme factory of 4chan and later 8chan that gave the alt-right its youthful energy, with its transgression and hacker tactics. The Guy Fawkes mask used in the protests in 2011 was a reference to Anonymous, which took its name, leaderless anti-celebrity ethic and networked style from the chaotic anonymous style of 4chan. V for Vendetta, which the Guy Fawkes mask is taken from, and the 'dark age of comic books' influenced the aesthetic sensibilities of this broad online culture.

While commentators praised the rejection of the right-left divide among a new wave of Internet-centric protest in the early 2010s, the political rootlessness of this networked, leaderless Internet-centric politics now seems a little less worthy of uncritical celebration. Anonymous activities have over the years leaned incoherently to the libertarian left and right, and everything in between, singling out everyone from Justin Bieber fans to feminists, fascists, cybersecurity specialists, and engaged in the kind of pervert-exposing vigilantism that blue-collar tabloid readers have long been mocked for.

To understand the seemingly contradictory politics of 4chan, Anonymous and its relationship to the alt-right, it is important to remember that the gradual right-wing turn in chan culture centered around the politics board /pol/, as compared to the less overtly political but always extreme 'random' board /b/. Along the way left-leaning 'moral fags' who had gravitated towards AnonOps IRCs suffered from a degree of state spying and repression during the height of Anonymous's public profile from around 2010 to 2012. This absence of the more libertarian left-leaning element within chan culture created a vacuum in the image boards that the rightist side of the culture was able to fill with their expert style of anti-PC shock humor memes.

4chan began with users sharing Japanese anime, created by a teenage Chris Poole (aka moot) and based on the anime-sharing site 2chan. Poole's main influence for the style of the site was inspired by a Something Awful subforum known as the Anime Death Tentacle Rape Whorehouse. It was set up in October 2003 and by 2011, it grew to around 750 million page views a month. New users were called newfags and older users oldfags. It became a massively influential and creative forum known for pranks, memes and images that 'cannot be unseen'. The culture of the site was not only deeply and shockingly misogynist, but also self-deprecating in its own self-mockery of nerdish 'beta' male identity. Cultural touchstones included war-based video games and films like *Fight Club* and *The Matrix*. There was no registration or login required, so posts were typically all under the username 'Anonymous'.

This culture of anonymity fostered an environment where the users went to air their darkest thoughts. Weird pornography, in-jokes, nerdish argot, gory images, suicidal, murderous and incestuous thoughts, racism and misogyny were characteristic of the environment created by this strange virtual experiment, but it was mostly funny memes. Poole has called 4chan a 'meme factory' and it undoubtedly created countless memes that made their way into mainstream Internet-culture. The most famous early examples of these were probably LOLcats, a cat-picture based style of image macro, and rickrolling, the use of a link to seemingly serious content that sends its user to a video of Rick

Astley singing *Never Gonna Give You Up*.

The users of 4chan/b/ acted collectively on things like making Chris Poole person of the year in Time magazine's online poll in 2008 and the collective cyber bullying of a random 11-year-old, Jessie Slaughter, in 2010. They got hold of her name and address, harassed her and encouraged her to commit suicide after she made a silly video of herself speaking in gangsta-rap style. Her situation was, unsurprisingly, not improved by her father posting a video in defence of his upset daughter, in which he threatened to call the 'cyberpolice'. In their emotionally underdeveloped way, lack of Internet-culture knowledge is always license on 4chan for any level of cruelty. They also acted collectively on less sinister pranks like Operation Birthday Boy, when an elderly man posted an online ad saying: 'people wanted for birthday party'. Touched by the lonely old man's appeal, they found his name, address and phone number, and sent him hundreds of birthday cards, and orders of cake and strippers.

In the *New York Times*, Mattathias Schwartz described 4chan/b/ like this:

> The anonymous denizens of 4chan's other boards — devoted to travel, fitness and several genres of pornography — refer to the /b/-dwellers as "/b/tards." Measured in terms of depravity, insularity and traffic-driven turnover, the culture of /b/ has little precedent. /b/ reads like the inside of a high-school bathroom stall, or an obscene telephone party line, or a blog with no posts and all comments filled with slang that you are too old to understand.

A common reference on the alt-right 'kek' started on 4chan and translated to 'lol' in comment boards on the multiplayer videogame *World of Warcraft*, while Pepe the Frog, originating in Matt Furie's Web comic *Boy's Club*, epitomizes online in-joke meme humor. Kek is also an ancient Egyptian deity represented as a frog-headed man while 'the Church of Kek' and 'praise Kek' refer to their ironic religion.

One of the things that linked the often nihilistic and ironic chan culture to a wider culture of the alt-right orbit was their opposition to political correctness, feminism, multiculturalism, etc., and its encroachment into their freewheeling world of anonymity and tech. In the US, one of the early cases of orchestrated attacks against such encroaching women was aimed at Kathy Sierra, a tech blogger and journalist. Sierra had been the keynote speaker at South by Southwest Interactive and her books were top sellers. The backlash against her was sparked when she supported a call to moderate reader comments, which at the time was seen as undermining the libertarian hacker ethic of absolute Internet freedom, although it has since become standard. Commenters on her blog began harassing and threatening her en mass, making the now routine rape and death threats received by women like Sierra. Personal details about her family and home address were posted online and hateful responses included photoshopped images of her with a noose beside her head, a shooting target pointed at her face and a creepy image of her being gagged with women's underwear. The personalized backlash against her was so extreme that she felt she had to close down her blog and withdraw from speaking engagements. When she explained on her blog why she had to step back from public life, writing that she was terrified that her stalkers might go through with their threats, it sparked a whole new wave of geek hatred against her.

Andrew Auernheimer (aka weev), a now well-known hacker and troll, seems to have been heavily involved in the attacks against Sierra, spreading false information online about her being a battered wife and a former prostitute. In 2009, weev claimed to have hacked into Amazon's system and reclassified books about homosexuality as porn. Once a part of the Occupy movement, he now regularly posts anti-Semitic and anti-gay rants on YouTube, has a swastika tattoo on his chest and was also the self-appointed president of a trolling initiative called the Gay Nigger Association of America. This was dedicated to opposing popular blogging and other mainstream activities, thought to be destroying authentic Internet-culture. Sierra has commented on how things have progressed: 'What happened to me pales in comparison to what's happening to women online today... I thought things would get better. Mostly, it's just gotten worse.'

Although online spaces and comment sections had started to develop a shocking level of woman-hatred years before, one of the early mainstream discussions of online misogynist extremism was sparked when Helen Lewis interviewed feminist writers in the *New Statesman*, who brought to light some of what they experienced. Feminist blogger and activist Cath Elliot wrote:

> If I'd been trying to keep a tally I would have lost count by now of the number of abusive comments I've received since I first started writing online back in 2007. And by abusive I don't mean comments that disagree with whatever I've written – I came up through the trade union movement don't forget, and I've worked in a men's prison, so I'm not some delicate flower who can't handle a bit of banter or heated debate – no, I'm talking about personal, usually sexualised abuse, the sort that on more than one occasion now has made me stop and wonder if what I'm doing is actually worth it. [...] I read about how I'm apparently too ugly for any man to want to rape, or I read graphic descriptions detailing precisely how certain implements should be shoved into one or more of my various orifices.

Feminist blogger Dawn Foster wrote:

> The worst instance of online abuse I've encountered happened when I blogged about the Julian Assange extradition case. [...] Initially it was shocking: in the space of a week, I received a

rabid email that included my home address, phone number and workplace address, included as a kind of threat. Then, after tweeting that I'd been waiting for a night bus for ages, someone replied that they hoped I'd get raped at the bus stop.

Feminist sex writer Petra Davis later wrote:

> When I started getting letters at my flat, I reported them to the police, but they advised me to stop writing provocative material. Eventually, I was sent an email directing me to a website advertising my services as a sex worker, with my address on the front page under the legend 'fuck her till she screams, filth whore, rape me all night cut me open', and some images of sexually mutilated women. It was very strange, sitting quietly in front of my screen looking at those images, knowing that the violence done to these other women was intended as a lesson... Of course, it didn't take long to take the site down, but by then I was thoroughly sick of the idea and more or less stopped writing about sex from any perspective.

Significant here is yet another cross-pollinating section of the broader alt-right milieu – masculinist and neomasculinist anti-feminist online subcultures. These are typically concerned with the decline of Western masculinity and some advocate things like the male separatism of Men Going Their Own Way (MGTOW), while others advise a more aggressive style of social-Darwinian informed pick-up artistry to 'game' the human system. But it was really the broadest orbit of the alt-right, which became known as the alt-light, that popularized this new diffuse and chaotic online set of cross-pollinating subcultures and helped bring it into the mainstream. These included social media celebrity figures like Milo, Twitter and blogging stars like Mike Cernovich, who wrote the male assertiveness guide *Gorilla Mindset*, former *Vice* editor

Gavin McInnes, and a host of Pepe meme-making gamers and 4chan-style shitposters, who had little in the way of a coherent commitment to conservative thought or politics but shared an anti-PC impulse and a common aesthetic sensibility. What we now call the alt-right is really this collection of lots of separate tendencies that grew semi-independently but which were joined under the banner of a bursting forth of anti-PC cultural politics through the culture wars of recent years. The irreverent trolling style associated with 4chan grew in popularity in response to the expanding identity politics of more feminine spaces like Tumblr. This, itself, spilled over eventually into 'real life' in the ramping up of campus politics around safe spaces and trigger warnings, 'gamergate' and many other battles.

One can feel the life draining out of the body at the thought of retelling or rereading the story of the gamergate controversy, one which involved internal controversies, hit pieces, hate campaigns, splits and a level of sustained high emotion more fitting for a response to a genocide than a spat over videogames. But for the sake of introduction here is a synopsis, which will undoubtedly satisfy neither side. In the lead-up to the gamergate controversy, feminist games critic Anita Sarkeesian found herself at the receiving end of a hate campaign like the Sierra case, but this time involving hundreds of thousands of participants and a level of vitriol utterly baffling to those outside of the gaming world, which lasted for several years. Her offence was creating a series of YouTube videos introducing viewers to some elementary concepts from feminist media criticism in an accessible and pretty mild-mannered style. Her level of criticism, as a self-identified games fan and someone who sought to reform rather than censor games, would be considered quite normal in literary or film criticism. These other audiences and critics are used to debate and to a relatively civilized adult kind of discourse, in which one can describe an old Hollywood classic as sexist without doubting its aesthetic value and one can disagree without going straight to the rape and death threats. Her videos feature no calls for video games to be censored or banned. They also offer no criticisms more harsh than what you might read from other pop-culture critics like Charlie Brooker or Mark Kermode on some very obviously retrograde depictions of women in *some* video games.

For this intolerable crime, Sarkeesian has endured years of jaw-droppingly dark and disturbing personal abuse. Typical online commentary has included things like: 'I'll rape you and put your head on a stick', 'It would be funny if five guys raped her right now', 'I violently masturbate to your face' and the old 4chan standard 'Tits or get the fuck out'. Her Wikipedia page was vandalized with pornographic images and hateful messages. There was also a campaign to mass report all of her social media accounts as spam, fraud or even terrorism.

Attempts were made to hack her website through a distributed denial of service (DDoS) attack and to hack into her email. Pornographic images of her being raped by video game characters were created and one offended male gamer even created a video game in which players could punch Anita's face until it was bloodied and bruised, and her eyes blackened and swollen. If you look up Anita today on YouTube you'll find countless videos devoted to hating her and obsessively trying to destroy her reputation and career. This was largely based on the fact that she ran a Kickstarter campaign that made more money than initially planned precisely because of the harassment. All of this was done, remember, to prove that sexism was *definitely not*, as she had so outrageously claimed, an issue in the 'gaming community'.

Tactics such as DDoS and doxxing (exposing the person's personal details to enable their mass harassment) used by 4chan and originating in Usenet culture became central to attacks by the anti-feminist gamers. Games marketed to the anti-feminist gamergate audience were more likely to aestheticize war, violence and technology, while in the years preceding gamergate, the market for games directed at women had grown. This was especially so with games like *Candy Crush*, aimed at teenage girls who don't know what *World of Warcraft* is and which obviously offended those who considered themselves real gamers. Gamergate itself kicked off when Zoe Quinn created a video game called *Depression Quest*, which even to a non-gamer like me looked like a terrible game featuring many of the fragility and mental illness-fetishizing characteristics of the kind of feminism that has emerged online in recent years. It was the kind of game, about depression, that would have worked as a perfect parody of everything the gamergaters hated about SJWs (social justice warriors).

Nevertheless, her dreadful game got positive reviews from politically sympathetic indie games journalists, which turned into a kind of catalyst for the whole gamergate saga. It was understood to be either a war over ethics in games journalism or an excuse to attack feminists and women entering the gamer world, depending on whom you ask. First, let me be clear on my own position on gaming. If you're an adult, I think you should probably be investing your emotional energies elsewhere. And that includes feminist gaming, which has always struck me as being about as appealing as feminist porn; in other words, not at all. However, anyone with some grasp on the basic norms of human conduct will still be able to see why the fallout was utterly unhinged based on Quinn's bad game, other cases of alleged biased reviews and what was no doubt an ideological project to change gaming to make some of it more feminist-friendly. It became possibly the biggest flame war in the history of the Internet so far, an overreaction on a grand scale, in which everyone accused everyone else of lying and malicious intent.

Eron Gjoni, Quinn's ex-boyfriend, posted on forums that she had cheated on him, setting off a wave of attacks on her in which she claims her haters began sending revenge porn to her family and employers, and trying to hack her accounts. Quinn was, needless to say, threatened with rape and death, and was doxxed. They then attacked a series of feminist gamers and games critics, who waded in, including Brianna Wu, Felicia Day and Jennifer Allaway. In each case there are countless conflicting accounts about the nature of threats and attacks, but even taking the uncontroversial ones alone, it is fair to say they did receive a level of abuse that in the pre-Internet days were reserved for few other than child murderers. This got so out of hand that even the founder of 4chan and champion of the anonymous Internet, moot, banned gamergate talk from 4chan, eventually causing him to leave the site, and the gamergaters moved to the more lawless 8chan.

Quinn found and recorded some of the conversations that took place on a 4chan IRC called 'burgersandfries', in which users conspired to destroy her career using the most extreme misogynist language and motivations. In this chat, they express their hatred and disgust towards her, and their glee at the thought of ruining her career. They also expressed fantasies about her being raped and killed. They hoped all the harassment would drive her to suicide and only the thought of 4chan getting bad publicity in response convinced some of them that this isn't something they should hope for. They distributed falsified nude pictures of her, posting links to online archives of them and sending them to Quinn's supporters. They attempted to dig up information about her family and to track down anyone with links to her. One found a picture of Quinn at age 13 and posted a link to it. So committed were they to ethics in games journalism that in this discussion they discuss Quinn's vagina as 'wide', large enough to 'fit 12 dicks at once' and 'a festering cheese-filled vagina' that leaves 'a trail of cunt slime' wherever she goes and then speculated about its smell.

Jenn Frank, an award-winning freelance games journalist, wrote an article entitled 'How to attack a woman who works in video gaming' for *The Guardian* that looked at on-going harassment. It outlined the ways in which trolls were harming women who work in the male-dominated field:

> ... someone recently and bafflingly tried to hack into my email and phone contacts. This is all very frightening to write, and so I must disclose that I *am* biased, insofar as I am terrified. I have worked in this industry for most of the last nine – not always perfect – years and I have never professed to be a perfect person. However, my values, my belief that abuse must not, cannot become 'normal', 'acceptable' or 'expected' is at odds with *oh, God, please, why are they doing this, what's the point, don't let it be me, don't let it be me*. My unabashed love for video games, my colleagues and my work have a conflict of interest with my own terror.

Games writer Jennifer Hepler also came under attacks, in which she claims to have been sent hundreds of abusive messages on Twitter, calling her things like an 'obese cunt' and threatening her. Feminist gamers complained that games writer Felicia Day was publicly dismissed as a 'booth babe' by a male games journalist. Games designer Patricia Hernandez drew the attention of 4chan, when she called it a 'cathedral of misogyny'. Encyclopedia Dramatica has a permanent entry for the memes 4chan created inspired by her comment, where she is described as:

> A fat, wetback 'game journalist' with sausage fingers and a chin like Jay Leno who works for Kotaku, a gaming gossip site infamous for allowing game designers to sleep with its columnists for good reviews and publicity. Patricia is a noted lesbian and feminazi who follows in Kotaku's proud tradition of writing countless articles about how various games either promote rape or literally rape their female players. Another

staple of Kotaku 'journalism' she takes part in is nepotism, which explains why every other article to come from her chubby hands is about her live-in girlfriend.

Without getting too far into the minutiae, and at this point it would be impossible to reach the end of all the various accusations of lies and contestations of how the mass event unfolded, the important feature of the furor here is the role it played in uniting different online groups and in spreading the tactics of chan culture to the broad online right. Gamergate brought gamers, rightist chan culture, anti-feminism and the online far right closer to mainstream discussion and it also politicized a broad group of young people, mostly boys, who organized tactics around the idea of fighting back against the culture war being waged by the cultural left. These included all kinds of people from critics of political correctness to those interested in the overreach of feminist cultural crusades. These brought in to the fold people like Christina Hoff Sommers, the classical liberal who started a video series called *The Factual Feminist,* which aimed to expose faulty statistics within feminism. Somewhere in the mix with the polite and light-hearted Sommers were also apolitical gamers, *South Park* conservatives, 4channers, hardline anti-feminists, and young people in the process of moving to the political far right without any of the moral baggage of conservatism. It also made Milo's ill-fated career, as he used it to shoot to mainstream celebrity status. Ultimately, the gamergaters were correct in their perception that a revived feminist movement was trying to change the culture and this was the front, their beloved games, that they chose to fight back on. The battle has since moved on to different issues with increasingly higher stakes, but this was the galvanizing issue that drew up the battle lines of the culture wars for a younger online generation.

The culture of 4chan, Anonymous etc., in the pre-gamergate days of Occupy and Anonymous could have gone another way.

Long before this 'geeks vs feminists' battle, the libertarian left had its own pro-hacker, pro-computer geek, Internet-centric political tradition, which some in the early Anonymous milieu obviously drew influence from. Hakim Bey's idea of the temporary autonomous zone was based on what he called 'pirate utopias' and he argued that the attempt to form a permanent culture or politics inevitably deteriorates into a structured system that stifles individual creativity. His language and ideas influenced anarchism and later, online cultures that advocated illegal downloading, anonymity, hacking and experiments like bitcoin. Echoes of John Perry Barlow's manifesto 'A Declaration of the Independence of Cyberspace' can be seen in this earlier period of Anon culture and in analyses that reflect a more radical horizontalist politics, like Gabriella Coleman's work. Barlow was one of the founders of the Electronic Frontier Foundation, anarchist hackers and defenders of an Internet free of state intervention, capitalist control and monopolizing of the online world. In a similar style to the rhetoric of 4chan and Anonymous ('we are legion'), it warned:

> Governments of the Industrial World, you weary giants of flesh and steel, I come from Cyberspace, the home of Mind. On behalf of the future I ask you of the past to leave us alone. You are not welcome among us. You have no sovereignty where we gather.

Instead, this leaderless anonymous online culture ended up becoming characterized by a particularly dark preoccupation with thwarted or failed white Western masculinity as a grand metaphor, which has had some 'real-life' manifestations. On 4chan a post, dated October 1, 2015, read:

> The first of our kind has struck fear into the hearts of America... This is only the beginning. The Beta Rebellion

has begun. Soon, more of our brothers will take up arms to become martyrs to this revolution.

The dramatic and knowingly cinematic tone was typical of the online style that hides itself from interpretation through a postmodern tonal distance, so that if any normie were to interpret it literally they would be laughed at. But in this case it was referring to the real news that a young man named Chris Harper-Mercer had killed nine classmates and injured nine others before shooting himself at Umpqua Community College in Roseburg, Oregon. The night before the shooting, a post on 4chan's /r9k/ board warned fellow commenters from the Northwestern United States to steer clear of school that day. The first responder in the thread asked: 'Is the beta uprising finally going down?' while others encouraged the anonymous poster and gave him tips on how to conduct a mass shooting.

In 2014, an anonymous 4chan user submitted several photos of what appeared to be a woman's naked and strangled corpse, along with a confession:

Turns out it's way harder to strangle someone to death than it looks on the movies... Her son will be home from school soon. He'll find her then call the cops. I just wanted to share the pics before they find me. I bought a bb gun that looks realistic enough. When they come, I'll pull it and it will be suicide by cop. I understand the doubts. Just check the fucking news. I have to lose my phone now.

Police later announced that the victim, Amber Lynn Coplin, was the woman in the photo. Her boyfriend, David Michael Kalac, was arrested after a brief police chase and charged with murder.

If further proof that the anti-PC taboo-breaking culture of 4chan is not just 'for the lulz' is needed, after the November 2015 shooting of five Black Lives Matter protesters in Minneapolis, a video emerged of two of the men involved, wearing balaclavas and driving to a Black Lives Matter protest, saying: 'We just wanted to give everyone a heads up on /pol/... Stay white.'

Just a few years ago the left-cyberutopians claimed that 'the disgust had become a network' and that establishment old media could no longer control politics, that the new public sphere was going to be based on leaderless user-generated social media. This network has indeed arrived, but it has helped to take the right, not the left, to power. Those on the left who fetishized the spontaneous leaderless Internet-centric network, declaring all other forms of doing politics old hat, failed to realize that the leaderless form actually told us little about the philosophical, moral or conceptual content of the movements involved. Into the vacuum of 'leaderlessness' almost anything could appear. No matter how networked, 'transgressive', social media savvy or non-hierarchical a movement may be, it is the content of its ideas that matter just as much as at any point in history, as Evgeny Morozov cautioned at the time. The online environment has undoubtedly allowed fringe ideas and movements to grow rapidly in influence and while these were left leaning it was tempting for politically sympathetic commentators to see it as a shiny new seductive shortcut to transcending our 'end of history'. What we've since witnessed instead is that this leaderless formation can express just about any ideology even, strange as it may seem, that of the far right.

## Chapter Two

# The online politics of transgression

Transgression has been embraced as a virtue within Western social liberalism ever since the 60s, typically applied today as it is in bell hooks' *Teaching to Transgress*. So elevated has the virtue of transgression become in the criticism of art, argued Kieran Cashell, that contemporary art critics have been faced with a challenge: 'either support transgression unconditionally or condemn the tendency and risk obsolescence amid suspicions of critical conservatism' as the great art critic Robert Hughes often was. But, Cashell wrote, on the value placed upon transgression in contemporary art: 'In the pursuit of the irrational, art has become negative, nasty and nihilistic.' Literary critic Anthony Julius has also noted the resulting 'unreflective contemporary endorsement of the transgressive'.

Those who claim that the new right-wing sensibility online today is just more of the same old right, undeserving of attention or differentiation, are wrong. Although it is constantly changing, in this important early stage of its appeal, its ability to assume the aesthetics of counterculture, transgression and nonconformity tells us many things about the nature of its appeal and about the liberal establishment it defines itself against. It has more in common with the 1968 left's slogan 'It is forbidden to forbid!' than it does with anything most recognize as part of any traditionalist right. Instead of interpreting it as part of other right-wing movements, conservative or libertarian, I would argue that the style being channelled by the Pepe meme-posting trolls and online transgressives follows a tradition that can be traced from the eighteenth-century writings of the Marquis de Sade, surviving through to the nineteenth-century Parisian avant-garde, the Surrealists, the rebel rejection of feminized conformity of post-war America and then to what film critics called 1990s 'male rampage films' like *American Psycho* and *Fight Club*.

Milo's favorite description of the unifying 'troll-y' sensibility across the new wave of the online right is 'transgressive'. Ever the unconvincing conservative, he would often say things like, 'the best sex is dangerous, transgressive, dirty' and that conservatism is the 'new punk' because it's 'transgressive, subversive, fun'. He regularly makes the comparison between punk and the alt-right, and obviously he's using the term in the broadest possible way. The ease with which this broader alt-right and alt-light milieu can use transgressive styles today shows how superficial and historically accidental it was that it ended up being in any way associated with the socialist left.

The use of the swastikas or Nazi flirtations as part of a performance certainly has precedents. Joy Division, whose singer Ian Curtis was on the political right, named themselves after the Freudenabteilung, the name of the German camp brothels in WWII. In 1976, in the company of the Sex Pistols, Siouxse Sioux was beaten up for wearing her swastika armband. Her intention was certainly to shock and offend, but few would argue that it was an earnest declaration of allegiance to Nazism. In post-WWII Britain, one can imagine the weight of the reverence toward the heroes who died fighting Nazism, and the suffering of many British citizens who lived through bombing raids and harsh years of economic austerity. At worst, the armband in this context can be seen as a brattish display of disrespect for its own sake. At best, it can be understood as a typically avant-garde style of transgressing taboos and as a two fingers to the post WWII establishment, who would use the heroism of the dead to stifle and repress dissent against queen and country.

In an interview with Esquire, weev/Auernheimer, with the swastika tattoo on his chest, explained his sensibility to the journalist:

I'm at a restaurant with Auernheimer and his friend Jaime Cochrane, who is a softly spoken transgender troll from the group Rustle League, so-called because 'that's what trolling is, it's rustling people's jimmies'. They're explaining to me their version of what trolls do. 'It's not bullying,' says Cochrane. 'It's satirical performance art.' Cyberbullies who drive teenagers to suicide have crossed the line. However, trolling is the more high-minded business of what Cochrane calls 'aggressive rhetoric', a tradition that goes back to Socrates, Jesus and the trickster god Loki, from Norse mythology. Auernheimer likens himself to Shakespeare's Puck. Cochrane aspires to Lenny Bruce and Andy Kaufman. They talk of culture jamming, the art of disrupting the status quo to make people think. They talk of Abbie Hoffman.

Significantly, the character of Patrick Bateman from the film adaptation of the novel *American Psycho* by Bret Easton Ellis has been one of the most common film references found on forums like 4chan and later the alt-right, alt-light and anti-feminist forums, along with *Fight Club* and *The Matrix*. The film tells the story of a narcissistic and sociopathic serial killer who watches pornography obsessively, is sexually violent to prostitutes, kills the homeless with relish and inflicts sexual torture on women in the novel so extreme it rivals de Sade in moral boundary pushing. Literary critic Daniel Fuchs has argued that the novel was part of a literary style, following on from Henry Miller and Norman Mailer, which used notions of transgression and sexual sovereignty from de Sade, and applied them as a form of rebellion and liberation through sexual aggression and violence. It is worth noting that one of the defenses made of *American Psycho* against its critics, during the debates sparked by its shocking sexual violence, was that the author had left some ambiguity at the end of the novel, suggesting that the events may have only been the crazed fantasies of the main character.

Just like the style of the rightist chan culture, interpretation and judgment are evaded through tricks and layers of metatextual self-awareness and irony.

The cult of the moral transgressor as a heroic individual is rooted in Romanticism. But, as Simon Reynolds and Joy Press explore in their study of post-war rebel masculinity *Sex Revolts*, it was revived in twentieth-century countercultures. Norman Mailer posited the psychopath as a noble and transgressive figure in fiction. He saw the hipster (which had somewhat different connotations at the time to the beard oil-applying variety of today) as borrowing from the tradition of the noble psychopath of fiction in his disregard for social conventions and the mainstream, and perceived the fictional psychopath as a symbol of being freed from sexual, social and moral inhibitions. The psychopath, like the artist, privileges id over superego and desire over moral constraints. Dostoyevsky's anti-hero in *Crime and Punishment*, Raskolnikov, asserted his own right to transcend the morality of the lesser masses when he killed a 'worthless' old woman. Echoed in the style of contemporary transgressive anti-moral cultures like 4chan that later fused with the alt-right, was French writer Maurice Blanchot's dictum that 'the greatest suffering of others always counts for less than my pleasure'.

Also in Press and Reynolds's analysis, from *One Flew Over the Cuckoo's Nest* to Michel Foucault's *Madness and Civilization* and R. D. Laing's *The Politics of Experience*, madness was consistently recast as nonconformity in this transgressive style. For de Sade, the Surrealists, and later for the 60s anti-repression cultural politics most closely associated with R. D. Laing, insanity was considered a creative source, a rejection of mainstream norms and a political act of rebellion. The surreal became a pre-rational creative expression. The throwing off of the id that characterized this transgressive countercultural traditional also characterized sites like 4chan, and its culture of trolling and taboo-breaking anti-moral humor, which is often described as insane or unhinged to baffled outsiders.

This view of psychopathy and rejection of imposed morality runs through the ethos and aesthetic of the rightist trolling culture. In one early self-description, a 4chan/b/ enthusiast wrote:

/b/ is the guy who tells the cripple ahead of him in line to hurry up. /b/ is first to get to the window to see the car accident outside. /b/ is the one who wrote your number on the mall's bathroom wall. /b/ is a failing student who makes passes at his young, attractive English teacher. /b/ is the guy loitering on Park Ave. that is always trying to sell you something. /b/ is the one who handed his jizz-drenched clothes to Good Will. (…) /b/ is a hot incest dream that you'll try to forget for days. /b/ is the only one of your group of friends to be secure in his sexuality and say anything. /b/ is the guy without ED who still likes trying Viagra. /b/ is the best friend that tags along for your first date and cock-blocks throughout the night. The decent girl you're trying to bag walks out on the date, /b/ laughs and takes you home when you're drunk, and you wake up to several hookers in your house who /b/ called for you. /b/ is a friend that constantly asks you to try mutual masturbation with him. /b/ is the guy who calls a suicide hotline to hit on the advisor. /b/ is nuking the hard-drive next time someone knocks on his door. /b/ is the one who left a used condom outside the schoolyard. /b/ is the voice in your head that tells you that it doesn't matter if she's drunk. /b/ is the friend who constantly talks about your mom's rack. /b/ is the only one who understands what the hell you saying. /b/ is someone who would pay a hooker to eat his ass, and only that. /b/ is the uncle who has touched you several times. /b/ is still recovering in the hospital, after trying something he saw in a hentai. /b/ is the pleasure you feel guilty of when you tried playing with your anus during masturbation. /b/ is wonderful.

The expression 'an hero' became part of chan slang. As Whitney Phillips recounts in her book *This Is Why We Can't Have Nice Things*, when a schoolboy from Minnesota called Mitchell Henderson shot himself, a message was left from a classmate on a MySpace memorial page read that Mitchell was 'an hero to take the shot, to leave us all behind. God do we wish we could take it back.' 4chan found this hilarious because of the mixture of the earnest emotional vulnerability and the grammatical error. There was also a reference on his memorial page to his lost iPod, which turned into a joke that became so elaborate that Henderson's MySpace page was hacked, while another placed an iPod on Henderson's grave, took a picture and posted it to 4chan. His face was pasted onto spinning iPods and hard-core porn scenes, and a re-enactment of Henderson's death soon appeared on YouTube, involving a shattered iPod. Mitchell's father received prank calls to his house, in which callers said things like: 'Hi, I've got Mitchell's iPod' and, 'Hi, I'm Mitchell's ghost, the front door is locked. Can you come down and let me in?'

Phillips also documented how when a US teenager called Chelsea King was raped and murdered, the Facebook pages devoted to finding her turned into memorial pages to mourn her and then trolling of these pages began, sometimes orchestrated on 4chan. Prank pages such as 'I bet this Pickle can get more fans than Chelsea King' were set up. Thus began a whole genre of trolling, generally referred to at the time as 'RIP trolling' emanating from 4chan's culture.

The forum's preoccupation with suicide, which became used as a verb to 'an hero', often takes the form of painful expressions of anonymous users' desire to commit suicide themselves, and at the same time it mocks suicide victims and those who express sympathy with the victims. Forum users come to the most arguably unsympathetic place imaginable to tell others of their suicidal fantasies anonymously, where they will probably be half-jokingly told to do it. They thus reject the perceived sentimentality of the mainstream media's suicide spectacles and instead remake it as their own dark spectacle, in which pity is replaced by cruelty. And yet, because both the act of suicide and the displays of insensitivity toward suicide victims are perceived as forms of transgression, both found a home within this strangely internally coherent online world. What other kind of ideas and styles are being drawn upon by this new transgressive rightist sensibility?

Nietzsche, one of the main thinkers being channeled by rightist chan culture knowingly or otherwise, argued for transgression of the pacifying moral order and instead for a celebration of life as the will to power. As a result, his ideas had appeal to everyone from the Nazis to feminists like Lily Braun. Today, the appeal of his anti-moralism is strong on the alt-right because their goals necessitate the repudiation of Christian codes that Nietzsche characterized as slave morality. Freud, on the other hand, characterized transgression as an anti-civilizational impulse, as part of the antagonism between the freedom of instinctual will and the necessary repressions of civilization. Perhaps the most significant theorist of transgression Georges Bataille inherited his idea of sovereignty from de Sade, stressing self-determination over obedience. Although rightist chan culture was undoubtedly not what Bataille had in mind, the politically fungible ideas and styles of these aesthetic transgressives are echoed in the porn-fuelled shocking content of early /b/ and in the later anti-liberal transgressions of the later /pol/. Bataille revered transgression in and of itself, and like de Sade viewed non-procreative sex as an expression of the sovereign against instrumentalism, what he called 'expenditure without reserve'. For him excessive behavior without purpose, which also characterizes the sensibility of contemporary meme culture in which enormous human effort is exerted with no obvious personal benefit, was paradigmatically transgressive in an age of Protestant instrumental rationality.

The culture that produced both Operation Birthday Boy and elaborate RIP page trolling became what you might call the unwanted gift, a twist on Mauss's *The Gift* that early Internet theorists used as a central metaphor for the non-instrumental culture of sharing that it nurtured. In *The Revolution of Everyday Life* by the Situationist thinker Raoul Vaneigem, Mauss's principle of the gift, originally used to describe reciprocal gift-giving systems in pre-modern societies, was celebrated on the grounds that only the purity of motiveless destruction or ruinous generosity can transcend instrumentalism. The Situationists' critique of 'the poverty of every day life', like Baudelaire's *An oasis of horror in a desert of boredom*, articulated a common sentiment found from the Romantics through to contemporary online cultures of transgression, that ennui, boredom and inertia requires a counterforce of extreme transgression. And yet these ideas often transcended the abstract. But while the Situationists had a better world in their hearts, the nihilistic application of the transgressive style already took shape in the 60s counterculture. 'The Manson murders', Reynolds and Press argued, 'were the logical culmination of throwing off the shackles of conscience and consciousness, the grim flowering of the id's voodoo energies.'

Another conceptualization of transgression that applies to this culture has been the idea of the carnivalesque. In *The Politics and Poetics of Transgression*, Stallybrass and White considered the carnivalesque to be a form of radical transgression against hierarchy and hegemony: 'The grotesque tends to operate as a critique of a dominant ideology which has already set the terms designating what is high and what is low.' This is very much how 4chan has long self-described and how it was described by its early 'progressive' boosters, except that the dominant ideology in the time of 4chan has been cultural liberalism, and the 'low' therefore meant un-PC poor taste, rudeness, shock, offence and trolling. The carnivalesque was also theorized by Bakhtin, whose ideologically flexible and ambivalent definition sounds much like some of the self-descriptions of trolls on what trolling is doing:

> Carnival laughter is the laughter of all the people. Second, it is universal in scope; it is directed at all and everyone, including the carnival's participants. The entire world is seen in its droll aspect, in its gay relativity. Third, this laughter is ambivalent; it is gay, triumphant, and at the same time mocking, deriding.

The transgressive style is not without precedent on the formally political conservative right, either. The Federation of Conservative Students in the UK famously shocked with a poster saying 'Hang Nelson Mandela' and criticized Thatcher for her soft touch, perhaps an early version of the 'cuckervative' jibe. They also had libertarian and authoritarian wings of thought, but certainly constituted a break from the decorum of the Burkeans, adopting some of the harder edge of the Thatcher era, even flirting with far-right ideas.

The reformist-left writer Christopher Lasch applied the Freudian conception of transgression as anti-civilizational to his critique of the vacuous nihilism and narcissism of post 60s American consumer society. But since the 60s the norm has until now been that critics of transgression have generally come from the right. Theorist of post-industrial society Daniel Bell lamented the transgressive ethos of the 60s and warned of its 'obsessive preoccupation with homosexuality, transvestism, buggery, and, most pervasive of all, publicly displayed oral-genital intercourse.' The transgressive irreverent style of the 60s counterculture was everything the right hated in previous culture wars. The 'adversary culture' bemoaned by conservative anti-feminists like Phyllis Schlafly and the neocons of *Commentary* magazine warned against the destructive impulses of the transgressive sensibility.

Feminism's relationship to the cultural politics of transgression is more complicated still. When the second wave of feminism burst forth in the 60s, captured in Betty Friedan's *The Feminine Mystique*, it was regarded by the right as part of the broader sexual revolution and the transgressive culture that was going to destroy the US family, moral restraints and tradition. In the battle over Roe vs Wade and Phyllis Schlafly's war on the Equal Rights Amendment, feminism was very much on the side of the transgressive tradition of de Sade, as it sought to destroy moralism and free the id. However, for some feminists the id of their transgressive male peers proved a little too free. Criticisms of the inequities of 'free love', and the hypocrisies and inequalities experienced by women in anti-war and other activist movements in the 60s and 70s, started to emerge from feminist writing as a kind of critique of the counterculture. The pornified culture produced by the sexual revolution soon came under its harshest criticisms from feminists like Andrea Dworkin and Catharine MacKinnon by the 80s, and soon the war-on-porn feminists even aligned with conservatives, who had previously denounced feminism as central to the debauchery of the 60s.

During the recent online culture wars, and their spillover into campus and protest politics, feminists have tried to embrace transgression with the Slut Walk movement and sex-positive pro-trans, pro-sex worker and pro-kink culture that was central to Tumblr. However, like the right, it has run up against a deep philosophical problem about the ideologically flexible, politically fungible, morally neutral nature of transgression as a style, which can characterize misogyny just as easily as it can sexual liberation. As Lasch understood, for progressive politics anti-moral transgression has always been a bargain with the devil, because the case for equality is essentially a moral one.

Equally hated and loved critic Camille Paglia argued that de Sade's depiction of human evil as innate was a form of satire directed against the Rousseauist tradition, from which contemporary feminism springs. De Sade's work famously features sexual violence as well as abhorrence for family and procreation, instead creating a violent transgressive sexuality based on the values of libertinism and individual sovereignty. In *Juliette* one rule of *The Sodality of the Friends of Crime* was, 'True libertinage abhors progeniture'. Paglia argued that de Sade's devaluing of the procreative female body, and his preoccupation with heterosexual and homosexual sodomy, also shared by chan culture, were not merely the product of a homosexual impulse, as argued by feminist Simone de Beauvoir, but a 'protest against relentlessly overabundant procreative nature'. Author Susan Suleiman wrote that:

The founding desire behind Sadeian fantasy is the active negation of the mother. The Sadeian hero's anti-naturalism goes hand in hand with his hatred of mothers, identified as the "natural" source of life.

That the transgressive values of de Sade could be taken up by a culture of misogyny and characterized an online anti-feminist movement that rejected traditional church-going conservatism should also not be a surprise. The Blakean motto adopted by the Surrealists, 'Sooner murder an infant in its cradle than nurse unacted desires', dominance as sexual 'sovereignty' and the freeing of the id from the constraints of the conscience have all descended from this transgressive tradition. Just as Nietzsche appealed to the Nazis as a way to formulate a right-wing anti-moralism, it is precisely the transgressive sensibility that is used to excuse and rationalize the utter dehumanization of women and ethnic minorities in the alt-right online sphere now. The culture of transgression they have produced liberates their conscience from having to take seriously the potential human cost of breaking the taboo against racial politics that has held since WWII. The Sadean transgressive element of the 60s, condemned by conservatives for decades as the very heart of the destruction of civilization, the degenerate and the nihilistic, is not being challenged by the emergence of this new online right. Instead, the emergence of this new online right is the full coming to fruition of the transgressive anti-moral style, its final detachment from any egalitarian philosophy of the left or Christian morality of the right.

## Chapter Three

# Gramscians of the alt-light

There were two major figures of the online culture wars Trumpian right who wrote glowingly about the hard core of the alt-right in a heavily quoted piece in *Breitbart* called 'An Establishment Conservative's Guide To The Alt-Right'. These were Milo Yiannopoulos and Allum Bokhari, who traced the intellectual roots of the amorphous alt-right back, in quite a flattering portrayal of the movement, to a number of key intellectuals and schools of thought. They singled out Oswald Spengler, the German philosopher who wrote *The Decline of the West* in 1918, who influenced the whole discourse of civilizational decline and advocated a nationalist non-Marxist socialism and authoritarianism, H. L. Mencken, the deeply elitist but undeniably brilliant anti-New Deal US satirist and cultural critic, who also made Nietzschean criticisms of religion and representative democracy, Julius Evola, the Italian philosopher loved by the Italian fascist movement, who advanced traditionalist and masculinist values and believed modern man lived in a Dark Age, Samuel Francis, the paleoconservative US columnist and critic of pro-capitalist neoconservatism and lastly, the French New Right, who importantly were sometimes called 'Gramscians of the right'.

The French New Right or Nouvelle Droite adapted the theories of Antonio Gramsci that political change follows cultural and social change. Andrew Breitbart's phrase was that politics is always 'downstream from culture', and was often quoted by Milo. Belgian far-right anti-immigration party Vlaams Blok leader Filip Dewinter put it like this: 'the ideological majority is more important than the parliamentary majority.'

Prior to 1968, the right had taken the view that 'ordinary

people' were still inherently conservative, which you can see echoed today in the 'silent majority' rhetoric of modern establishment conservatives. The French New Right's Gramscian aim, which the alt-right today also shares, was to break with the view that defeat of radical elites or vanguards would enable the restoration of a popular traditional order and instead took stock of how profoundly the 60s had changed the general population and become hegemonic.

As Andrew Hartman outlined in his book on the 90s culture wars, *The War for the Soul of America*, the radical upheavals of Paris 1968 and the rise of the New Left was proof to the demoralized right that the whole culture would now have to be retaken before formal political change could come. This led to the pursuit of a 'metapolitics', and a rejection of the political party and traditional activism within a section of the right. Instead, they set about rethinking their philosophical foundations and creating new ways to counter the '68 ideology of Social Progress. The resulting French New Right shared many of the alt-right's preoccupations like multiculturalism and imminent Western decline, also drawing on and adapting ideas from across the political spectrum. For example, they had a strong critique of capitalism, promoting instead local 'organic democracy'.

Today, the movement that has been most remarkably successful at changing the culture rather than the formal politics is the alt-light. They were the youthful bridge between the alt-right and mainstream Trumpism. Although the tactics of the online right are updated to a digital age, it is hard to think of a better term than Gramscian to describe what they have strategically achieved, as a movement almost entirely based on influencing culture and shifting the Overton window through media and culture, not just formal politics.

They succeeded largely by bypassing the dying mainstream media and creating an Internet-culture and alternative media of their own from the ground up. Here, I want to look more closely at those being called the alt-light, who became major independent social media figures with huge audiences well before Trump's win. They influenced Internet-culture and eventually more mainstream culture. How did they do this and why did it work?

First, think for a moment about the amount of scholarly and polemical writing that has come from a broadly left perspective in recent generations, attempting to explain why it is that the project of the revolutionary socialist left continues to fail and remains unpopular. Entire schools of thought about the culture industry, media hegemony, discourse, narrative, normativity and power have this problem either overtly or implicitly at their core. Edward Herman and Noam Chomsky's 'manufacturing consent' thesis has remained quite dominant in left rhetoric ever since it was written. The Frankfurt School and the Situationists remain canonical in university theory courses. Of all the Marxian and Marxoid schools of thought, Gramsci's is perhaps the most influential today, placing media and culture at the center of political analysis and praxis in a mediated age after the decline of the old labour movement.

And yet at the end of 2016 it was the candidate of the right, Donald Trump, who was elected President of the United States despite all mainstream news agencies, including conservative media from Fox News to National Review, working openly against him. Figures like Milo, who were being dismissed as an irrelevant Internet fringe despite their growing mass online audiences right up until the election results came in, rose to mainstream success along with him.

Let's also remember that during the Obama years millennial cultural liberals had their own new media platforms to fill the vacuum left by the decline in the centrality of mainstream newspapers and TV as the general arena for public discourse. In this brave new world of clicks and content, their alternative came in the form of the often-sentimental feel-good clickbait sites like Upworthy and listicle sites like Buzzfeed. Other liberal sites like Everyday Feminism, Jezebel and Salon delivered a strange mixture of ultra-sensitivity, sentimentality and what was once considered radical social constructionist identity politics.

These sites ran headlines that became almost self-satirizing like '8 Signs Your Yoga Practice Is Culturally Appropriated', 'Men can be feminists but it's really hard work', '19 Of The Most Totally Amazing Body-Shaming Clap Backs' and many others on toxic masculinity, fat pride, gender-neutral toys and quandaries about moral and culturally sensitive consumerism. Clickhole, a project of The Onion, emerged as a timely satirical site that brilliantly mocked the liberal clickbait style with inane titles like: '10 Things People With a Spider On Their Face Are Tired of Hearing' and 'Our Country Has Become Worryingly Desensitized To Violence In Hot-Sauce Names'.

Unintentionally amusing and easily satirized as sites like Upworthy may have been, at its height in 2013 it was averaging about 75,000 Facebook likes per article, while its site traffic was coming in at around 87 million unique visitors per month. In 2015, the liberal listicle site Buzzfeed's articles were getting more shares on social media than BBC and Fox News put together. All of these were liberal, millennial-oriented and openly propagandistic.

While the alt-right regard these and the Guardian, BBC and CNN as the media of 'the left', espousing 'Cultural Marxism', it became obvious when the possibility of any kind of economically 'left' political force emerged that liberal media sources were often the most vicious and oppositional. Liberal feminist journalist Joan Walsh called Bernie Sanders's supporters 'Berniebot keyboard warriors', while Salon was one of the main propagators of the Berniebro meme with headlines like, 'Bernie Bros out of control: Explosion of misogynist rage…' and, 'Just like a Bernie Bro, Sanders bullies Clinton…' Meanwhile *Vice*, a magazine that made its brand on the most degenerate combination of vacuous hipster aesthetics and pornified transgression, published things like 'How to spot a brocialist'. Before the elections *The Guardian* newspaper ran a piece with the comically cultish wording: 'Time to hail Hillary Clinton – and face down the testosterone left'.

Despite overwhelming evidence of Bernie's popularity among young women, the myth was relentlessly peddled until it passed into the realm of Internet truth. The old liberal establishment then weighed in; for example, when feminist Gloria Steinem claimed that these numerous female Bernie fans were merely trying to impress their male peers. In the UK, an almost identical phenomenon occurred when the British liberal media establishment, particularly *The Guardian,* joined forces with their more youthful online offspring in smearing Corbyn and his supporters as being motivated primarily by this nefarious tide of brocialism, despite his squeaky-clean track record on women's issues in the UK.

Where, then, was the real left's alternative media during this period? On YouTube, *The Young Turks* emerged as one of the few genuinely popular talk-show platform video producers, with 3 million subscribers and typical video views of 100,000 to 200,000. British Laborite Owen Jones started producing popular interview videos. Further to the left, *Jacobin* magazine was undoubtedly the success story of this period in print publishing and certainly the most interesting media project intellectually. This is because it gave a platform to left critics of the liberal Hillary-supporting center left like Adolph Reed, Walter Benn Michaels, Amber A'Lee Frost, Connor Kilpatrick, Liza Featherstone and many others. Inevitably *Jacobin*, too, was smeared for being the magazine of choice for Bros and 'the white left', despite its two key founders being the children of Jamaican and Trinidadian immigrants, and of having its logo based on the Black Jacobin.

In 2016, the podcast Chapo Trap House also emerged as a form of left comedy, which specialized in mocking the most absurd outer limits of online identity politics of the right and to a lesser degree, the liberal left. In the UK, *Novara Media* had a relatively small following but produced short and sharp video content, which few on the left have been doing, giving voice to British black and Asian left voices from a London-based multicultural point of view. Current Affairs was also a small but important left-wing print project that critiqued the liberal left as well as the right.

But what few on the left were paying attention to in the years leading up to Trump's election, and really throughout the entire Obama administration, was the alt-light building a multilayered alternative online media empire that would dwarf many of the above. This stretched from white nationalist bloggers in its sparsely populated corners to the charismatic YouTubers and Twitter celebrities in its more popular form. These included right-wing outsiders such as Steve Bannon who, through building a publication like *Breitbart*, became chief strategist to the US president.

YouTube vloggers produced an abundance of popular commentary videos and 'SJW cringe compilations', while alt-light celebrities like Milo built careers from exposing the absurdities of the kind of Tumblr identity politics that had gone mainstream through listicle sites like Buzzfeed and anti-free speech safe space campus politics. Meanwhile, ironic meme-making adolescent shitposters formed a reserve army of often darkly funny chan-style image-based content producers, who could be easily summoned in moments like gamergate or whenever big figures like Milo needed backup, to swarm and harass their opposition.

Since 2015, the Canadian conservative project The Rebel Media produced high production value video shows for YouTube. Some big names included Gavin McInnes, former editor of *Vice* magazine, and Lauren Southern, who specialized in filming Vox Pops at SlutWalks and campus protests, in which she challenged the protesters in a mocking style that reminded me very much of the genre perfected by liberal media during the rise of the Tea Party movement, in which the interviewees were always made to look stupid. Led by Ezra Levant, formerly from the conservative *Sun News* network, the move was designed to cut costs and go exclusively online unencumbered by TV regulations. To launch the YouTube channel a crowdfunding campaign raised around $100,000 (Canadian dollars) and then launched a pay service of $8.00 per month for access to all the media outlet's YouTube shows. After the elections, The Rebel announced they had recorded 19 million video views in a 30-day period. On an average day, according to their official figures, more than 600,000 people watch Rebel videos. These figures are even a low estimate when you take into account the amount of reposted material sourced from Rebel appearing on other YouTube channels.

Gavin McInnes' subscriber show on Rebel called *How's It Goin', Eh?* mixed politics and comedy. His free-to-view shows typically featured a 10-minute piece about current events in the culture wars. McInnes, who was born in England to Scottish parents, has a kind of *South Park* conservative political sensibility. He started his creative life in a punk band called Anal Chinook and now calls himself a 'free-market capitalist' and 'anarchist' with a somewhat unconvincing or at least conflicted moral conservative streak. He advocates porn abstinence and traditional marriage, despite using the kind of vulgar sexual language that many of his conservative role models would have had his show banned for in previous culture wars. His role as an editor at *Vice* led to him being referred to as one of the 'primary architects of hipsterdom', but he went on to make his name on the right through his anti-feminist arguments that life in the modern workplace had made women miserable and that the dominant media ideology teaches women to be fat, single and childless. He had to step down as chief creative officer of Rooster, an advertising agency start-up he cofounded, following the publication of an essay entitled 'Transphobia is Perfectly

Natural'.

Lauren Southern, the other major star of Rebel who later went independent, rose to fame when she attended a SlutWalk in Vancouver with the sign 'There Is No Rape Culture In The West'. She was perfect for Vox Pops as a telegenic young blonde woman with a sarcastic disapproving tone of voice. At another protest, Southern shouted 'there are only two genders', before a protester poured a container of urine over her head. Southern was also heavily involved in 'The Triggering' in response to International Women's Day, in which anti-feminist Twitter users posted intentionally offensive content to assert their right to free speech online. At the time of writing, one reposted version of her protest footage that popped up in my YouTube recommendations called 'Social Justice Warriors Piss On Your Free Speech – Lauren Southern Attacked' had nearly 500,000 views. She has 235,000 followers on Twitter and occasionally appears on mainstream news media like Sky News, where she was kicked off live on air for saying:

I don't know why legal immigration even exists anymore. I could just put on some bronzer, get on a dinghy boat and show up on the border of Sicily or the beaches of Sicily with a Koran in hand and be accepted as an immigrant. Or go across the border with Caracas and be accepted as an immigrant.

*Breitbart* has been one of the key players in the Trumpian right culture war, a conservative website founded as recently as 2007 by conservative commentator Andrew Breitbart. It also has a daily radio program called *Breitbart News Daily*. It is perhaps the single biggest success story of right-wing alternative media, with celebrities like Milo, its editor Steve Bannon rising to the top of US politics and its staff writers rising from relative obscurity to having meetings with the president. Bannon himself described the site as a 'platform for the alt-right', though he undoubtedly meant this in the looser sense of a new anti-establishment right, aligned with the European populist right and the US Trumpian right.

After the election, Buzzfeed published a transcript of a long interview Steve Bannon gave to the Vatican from 2004. Presumably thinking this was a ready-made hit-piece that would destroy his reputation, Bannon came across in the interview as darkly fascinating and, relative to many Buzzfeed listicle writers, as quite a serious and intriguing person. He spoke of 'the crisis of capitalism', secularization, the Islamization of the West, the immorality of crony capitalism and the destruction of the West's Judeo-Christian heritage. Contrary to what Buzzfeed may have intended, it revealed a thinker who could not be further from the neoconservative or neoliberal establishments within the two major US parties, but instead as an anti-establishment figure with ambitious ideas.

Ben Shapiro was a key media figure to leave *Breitbart* over its flirtations with the anti-Semitic hard alt-right. Shapiro wrote that under Bannon's leadership, '*Breitbart* has become the alt-right go-to website… pushing white ethno-nationalism as a legitimate response to political correctness, and the comment section turning into a cesspool for white supremacist mememakers.' This sparked an anti-Semitic hate campaign against Shapiro, which he strongly implied was actively encouraged by Milo. After his second son was born, Shapiro received tweets and comments with wishes that 'all 4 of you will go to the ovens'. Among Milo's many digs at Shapiro, he tweeted a photo of a black baby at him after his son was born and wrote, 'Prayers to Ben who had to see his baby come out half-black. And already taller than he is!' – a reference to his new status as a 'cuckservative'.

Cathy Young, a Russian Jewish US citizen, a libertarian commentator and writer for *Reason* magazine, had once been a fellow traveler of Milo and gamergate. However, she went on to cut ties with anyone too close to the alt-right as she began to see the same anti-Semitic and sinister elements grow and go unchallenged by those whose ascendant careers depended upon not punching right. At the time Milo's star was ascending, everyone wanted to know about some youth movement called the alt-right and he was enraged by her principled position when she and Milo were interviewed on BBC radio. His fans mocked and abused her but today, since Milo's career has been destroyed, to the indifference or even glee of the alt-right he was promoting, Young has emerged with her dignity intact, as the much wiser and more principled, astute critic.

Milo was undoubtedly the biggest star to emerge from the rise of the Trumpian online right. The British gay commentator started as a young and more recognizably conservative figure using the pseudonym Milo Andreas Wagner. In an early TV appearance on the *10 O'clock Show* in the UK, a young, slightly shy, brown-haired Milo, dressed like someone from a *Belle and Sebastian* video, discussed gay marriage with Boy George and the host David Mitchell. He was introduced as a conservative Catholic. At that stage he hadn't quite found his brand and it would have been impossible to know what a star he would become. He later founded *The Kernel*, an online tabloid magazine about technology, reinventing himself as a much more modern kind of tech and culture writer. He achieved mainstream fame and celebrity status in 2014, when he sympathetically covered gamergate. Milo has done more than anyone else to give the alt-right a presentable face, giving even their worst fascistic incarnations positive coverage, despite himself being Jewish, gay, etc. Right before the scandal that ended his career, he had appeared on Bill Maher's show and had signed a $250,000 book deal.

His real media achievement in terms of Gramscian-right tactics and thinking was his Dangerous Faggot Tour. If you watched a live stream of the tour the live comments section quickly filled up little walls, swastikas and references to Harambe. These videos were viewed typically hundreds of thousands of times, as he visited US and UK universities criticizing political correctness, feminism, Islam, Black Lives Matter and Western liberalism in general. Through courting online controversy and campus activists constantly trying to ban him, he was made into a kind of martyr figure, with devoted crowds of fans chanting 'Milo! Milo! Milo!' His ban from Twitter aided his career in much the same way. As for genuine non-ironic white supremacists on the alt-right, he insisted: 'There's just not very many of them, no-one really likes them, and they're unlikely to achieve anything significant in the alt-right.' Just a few months later, Milo's career was destroyed seemingly by the right itself as a years-old clip from an interview in which he defended pederasty was dredged up and many of the staff at *Breitbart* said they would quit if he was not fired from the magazine as a result. The hard alt-right who he said would never have influence are now stronger and more confident than ever, while his career is in free fall, and after the revelations came out Richard Spencer tweeted 'Milo's done. Put a fork in him.'

Mike Cernovich is another major figure in the alt-light milieu, who currently has 222,000 followers on Twitter and has published popular guides to right-wing politics and male assertiveness, Gorilla Mindset and MAGA Mindset. He developed his media profile through Twitter, periscope videos and blogging at the website Danger and Play, a reference to Nietzsche's famous quote, 'The true man wants two things: danger and play. For that reason he wants woman, as the most dangerous plaything.' A profile written in the *New Yorker* claimed that he launched Danger and Play after his first wife filed for divorce and that they had been law students together. After law school, his wife became a successful attorney in Silicon Valley, while Cernovich was not admitted to the California bar until nine years after getting his law degree. Cernovich admitted that his wife earned millions of dollars in stocks and that he received 'seven figures' of her money in the divorce settlement, which explains his ability to build an independent media career.

Another important figure in this milieu is conspiracy theorist Alex Jones, founder of Infowars, whose tagline is: 'There's a war on for your mind!' *The Alex Jones Show* airs on the radio across the US and online. He has accused the US government of orchestrating the Oklahoma City bombing, the September 11th attacks and a fake moon landing. Somewhat like a right-wing version of the anti-capitalist anti-globalization movement the rose up in the 90s, he believes that globalists have colluded to create a New World Order. The Southern Poverty Law Center describes him as 'the most prolific conspiracy theorist in contemporary America' and though his crazed shirt-ripping style is easy to laugh at, his YouTube channel gets millions of viewers, now reaching a mainstream audience.

One of the only strictly alt-right figures to rival the popularity and mainstream media attention of the alt-light, though later and in part as a result of their initial success, was Richard Spencer. He effectively coined the term alt-right and made the 'red pilled' metaphor more common across the broad Trumpian right. Spencer has said, 'Race is something between a breed and an actual species' and believes non-white Americans should leave in a 'peaceful ethnic cleansing'. He held a certain fascination for the media as the full ugliness and horror of the alt-right was exposed after Trump's election. This was in part because he was surprisingly young, even 'dapper', articulate and well dressed for an Internet fascist – obviously a modest compliment, but he was certainly far from the typical 'neckbeard' stereotype.

Spencer believes the alt-right will continue to infiltrate mainstream US formal politics through culture, starting with a focus on deporting undocumented immigrants under Trump, later moving on to negative migration as a goal and eventually on to a white ethnostate. He once told Mother Jones: 'Conservatism is going to be dead in my lifetime and the question is, who is going to define the right after that? I want to do that.' Spencer started out as a scholar of Leo Strauss and his MA thesis was on Adorno and Wagner, but he later dropped out of his Duke University Ph.D. You can still detect in his writing and public speeches that he longs for a more intellectual European style of blood and soil nationalism and he said in an interview that he used to want to be an avant-garde theater director. He speaks with spitting disdain about the vulgarity of the US consumer culture-loving, Big-Mac munching, Bush-voting, pick-up truck owning pro-war Republican style. His writing style comes across as that of a person who might wear surgical gloves when leaving the house.

Spencer had worked at *The American Conservative*, a high-quality anti-war anti-establishment conservative magazine, before being fired for his extreme views and moving to *Taki's Magazine*, where he used the term 'alt-right' regularly. After Hillary named the alt-right in a speech during the elections, Spencer finally achieved mainstream media exposure, featuring especially in liberal left-leaning publications like *Vice*.

Spencer regards Trump as someone who will accelerate the collapse of US multicultural feminist liberalism, calling him after his election 'the Napoleon of the current year'. When Trump got elected, in the first national meeting of his organization the National Policy Institute, Spencer saluted the crowd of about 300 people with 'Hail Trump, hail our people, hail victory!' as a few crowd members did a Nazi salute. Interestingly though, this overt declaration of the alt-right Trump alliance as a fascist or at least far-right racial project sparked anger among some alt-light figures like Mike Cernovich, who came out against Spencer and his online followers, saying that Spencer was part of a government project of 'controlled opposition' – a plant presumably used to discredit all opposition to establishment Republican Party neoconservatism as fascist. Cernovich broke from the alt-right code 'don't punch to the right' after the footage of Spencer and his followers blew up. He insulted the entire core of the white nationalist alt-right, calling anti-Semite public figure David Duke a 'reprobate gambler' and 'conman'.

While this disparate set of young rightist social media celebrities was held together through pure hatred of their opposition in the mainstream media and the political center, the divisions within the broader orbit of the alt-right started to appear almost instantly, with the success of Trump and their sudden mainstream exposure. This is of course an old story that should be familiar to anyone who knows the history of any marginal political movements that suddenly achieve mainstream success. Their Gramscian strategy has been successful beyond any predictions; though much of it emerged from the chaos of a crumbling political and media mainstream.

One thing that can't be denied is their remarkable success in spreading their ideas through their own alternative and almost exclusively online media content in the absence of traditional media, political establishment bodies or other institutional support. It appears as though in the online culture wars, those heeding the ideas of the left most closely, from Chomsky's idea of manufacturing consent to Gramsci's theory of hegemony and counter-hegemony, and applying them most strategically, were the right.

## Chapter Four

# Conservative culture wars from Buchanan to Yiannopoulos

Where does the most mainstream wing of the alt-right – the alt-light – fit historically in terms of its political ideas and style? Throughout the US presidential race, Milo Yiannopoulos regularly reiterated that he loved 'Daddy' (Donald Trump), because he was 'the first truly cultural candidate since Pat Buchanan'. He admitted in a *Bloomberg* profile that he doesn't 'care about politics' and has reiterated this point explicitly on several occasions, but is instead interested in the cultural battles that are shaping it.

It seems to me that politics, on the contrary, has been hollowed out too much into *little other* than a purely cultural politics over the last half-century, which the ugly spectacle of the Trump-Hillary race represented the logical conclusion of – politics as culture war. It was just that until Trump and the emergence of the new online right, the liberals had been resoundingly winning. In this style of politics, what a political leader actually does often seems entirely secondary to what cultural politics they profess to have. In modern politics, liberal leaders are forgiven for drone bombing as long as they're cool with gay marriage, while on the right, enacting policies that devastate families and stable communities was cheered on at any cost as long as it dealt a satisfying blow to the trade unions, as we saw during the Reagan and Thatcher years. For both Yiannopoulos and his online liberal enemies in the culture wars, essentially two rival wings of contemporary identity politics, to be said to have purely cultural politics would not be considered particularly pejorative.

Nevertheless, Yiannopoulos's comparison is an interesting one. Buchanan is perhaps most famous for his declaration of 'a war for the soul of America' during his famous speech before the 1992 Republican National Convention. In his invocation of Buchanan, Yiannopoulos was drawing a parallel between his own anti-PC Trumpian culture war online and that of the conservative culture war of the 90s. Buchanan's speech was itself a delayed backlash to the previous culture war of the 60s and the devastating cultural losses suffered by conservatives that resulted.

In positioning his own highly mediated war with the new wave of identity politics sweeping the Anglophone world in recent years as the contemporary equivalent of Buchanan's, Yiannopoulos was weaving himself into a broader historic narrative. In this narrative, he and the new online Trumpian trolling right are leading another great push, as important as the culture wars of the 60s and of the 90s, only this time with a bit of youth and Internet subcultural cool on their side. Whether his career can survive the incriminating interview in which he defended pederasty remains to be seen, but he played an enormously important role in the culture wars that shaped the period in the years leading up to the election of Trump. So, looking at his statements and speeches on his Dangerous Faggot Tour and Buchanan's, how much do each of their culture wars really have in common?

Buchanan's book *Death of The West* has been hugely influential on the paleoconservative ideas that have rivaled those of the pro-market modernizing neocons. He called neoconservatism 'a globalist, interventionist, open borders ideology.' Through American Conservative, he and other like-minded anti-establishment conservatives opposed the Iraq War and took many other positions that distinguished them from the internationalist, free market, and pro-interventionist components of the right. Long before Trump's election Buchanan was talking about the white working class as naturally conservative, opposed globalization and neoliberal trade deals, and pushed for a crack down on immigration. While the neocons had their origins in the materialism of the anti-Soviet left, Buchanan also stressed the non-material questions of patriotism, the nation, family, community and cultural inheritance.

With some reservations he supported Trump saying: 'The idea of economic nationalism, an end to globalism, putting America first in trade, securing the border, one nation, one people—I'm still a conservative Republican, but this is the new and enlarged agenda.' When asked if he considered himself connected to the alt-right, he said: 'They're much younger, they're basically guys in their twenties and thirties. Some people I know walked out of it—they're not into *Sieg Heil*, they're not into this stuff... the media loves this stuff, they can't get enough of it.'

The conservative culture war of the 90s had tried to push back against the enormous gains of the cultural left over abortion, affirmative action, art, censorship, evolution, family values, feminism, pornography and the Western canon. Buchanan's style was more pugilistic than most of the Republican mainstream was willing to risk and his culture war speech remains an undeniably brilliant piece of writing and oratory, as well as one of the most important speeches in US history. The speech was a defense of Ronald Reagan and, after losing the presidential nomination himself, a defense of the Republican nominee George Bush senior. But primarily it was really a call to engage in a larger culture war: 'There is a religious war going on in this country. It is a cultural war, as critical to the kind of nation we shall be as was the Cold War itself, for this war is for the soul of America.'

The right-wing style that Yiannopoulos embodied represents a marriage of the ironic, irreverent, taboo-busting culture of 4chan with the politics of the right; although, as his hard alt-right detractors often liked to point out, once you remove the 'trolling', many of his views amount to little more than classical liberalism. Despite calling himself a conservative he, Trump, rightist 4chan and the alt-right all represent a pretty dramatic departure from the kind of churchgoing, upstanding, button-down, family-values conservatism that we usually associate with the term in Anglo-American public and political life. As a bursting forth of the id unrestrained by conventions of speech or PC culture, the whole online sensibility is more in the spirit of foul-mouthed comment-thread trolls than it is of Bible study, more *Fight Club* than family values, more in line with the Marquis de Sade than Edmund Burke. It is sometimes said that the right won the economic war and the left won the culture war. And as political theorist Walter Benn Michaels has argued, it is the recognition of identity that has triumphed over economic equality as the organizing principle of the Anglo-American liberal left and of mainstream discourse more broadly.

In full agreement with him, I would also argue that the most recent rise of the online right is evidence of the triumph of the identity politics of the right and of the co-opting (but nevertheless the triumph) of 60s left styles of transgression and counterculture. The libertinism, individualism, bourgeois bohemianism, postmodernism, irony and ultimately the nihilism that the left was once accused of by the right actually characterized the movement to which Milo belonged. The rise of Milo's 4chan-influenced right is no more evidence of a resurgence of conservatism than the rise of Tumblr-style identity politics constitutes a resurgence of the socialist or materialist left.

As Andrew Hartman writes in *A War for the Soul of America*, in Buchanan's speech the invocation of the fall of Soviet Communism indicated how at the end of the Cold War the Soviet enemy *without* had become the bohemian, transgressive, permissive enemy *within* for the US right. Reagan had overseen the defeat of the Soviet Union, the speech suggested, but more important now was the defeat of what had come out of the 60s, including what critic Lionel Trilling called 'adversary culture' within the West itself.

The 60s were bitterly remembered by conservatives like

Buchanan, when counterculture brought the bohemian styles of the Beats to the mainstream and student revolts broke out from Paris to California. Trilling's 'adversary culture', an idea that preoccupied the right at the time, meant a political or intellectual culture that sought to counter and subvert the existing order, and smash that which went before, often through irreverence and transgression for transgression's sake, and later in the more respectable world of academia. Though it became a term to describe the post-60s academic takeover, it is remarkably similar to how Yiannopoulos himself was described as he rose to prominence (transgressive, subversive, speaking truth to power, exposing lies, etc.) even as he identified academe as the problem at the root of millennial cultural liberalism.

Many of the key thinkers of the 60s moment were interested in something that later characterized the online irreverent anti-PC right – non-conformism. In his book *White Collar: The American Middle Classes*, C. Wright Mills depicted the post-war US as a dystopian iron cage of conformity. His readers envisioned an alternative or antidote by creating a counterculture of non-conformity, individuality and rebellion. Another hugely influential anti-conformist thinker of the time, Paul Goodman, advocated anti-authoritarianism, experimental psychology and a rejection of social restrictions and taboos in *Growing Up Absurd: The Problems of Youth in the Organized Society*. Antipathy to duty, the work ethic, the bureaucratic straightjacket, the company man, the square, had come from the Beats, and fused with the anti-war and student movements to form the New Left.

It is significant here too that, despite the constant accusations of 'Cultural Marxism' by the Trumpian online right, the countercultural aesthetics of anti-conformism in the US were later cultivated by the US government as part of a culture war against communism. Through the Congress for Cultural Freedom, a covert cultural soft-power initiative, it was the Cold War anti-communist liberals who used non-conformism, self-expression and individualism to rival the collectivist, conformist, productivist and heavily restricted Soviet Union, which still revered the uniformed pre-60s anti-individualist forms of culture like army choirs, marching bands, orchestras and ballet. By the time Buchanan gave his speech in 1992, the Cold War was over and the economic program of the Western democratic left had suffered a catastrophic defeat during the Reagan and Thatcher years. However, the socially and morally permissive, transgressive, nonconformist cultural project within the US New Left had by then emerged triumphant and, as it turned out, coexisted quite comfortably with the scorched-earth free-market economics of the right – a fusion that reached its fullest expression in the Blair/Clinton era, when a non-conformist cultural gesture could still cover a multitude of economic sins.

Recent online culture wars have reopened many fault lines within the right as well as the left. Anti-Trump conservatives of today are deemed 'cuckservatives' by the alt-right, the passive cuckolding husband to the rapacious non-white foreign enemy at the gates. The neocon and old-fashioned Christian right is hated in this way by the alt-right for, in one way or another, failing to protect the nation aggressively enough, by playing too nicely and thus not being up to the job of defeating feminism, Islamification, mass immigration and so on. In stark contrast to the Pepe-posters and potty-mouthed Milo fans would be someone like British conservative columnist Peter Hitchens, for example, who called Trump 'this yahoo, this bully, this groper, a man who threatened his opponent with jail... I loathe Mr. Trump for his coarseness, his crudity, and his scorn for morals, tradition and law.' In this sense Trump remains closer to the sensibilities of Yiannopoulos and the trolling online right than he does to conservatism or to something like *National Review* magazine, founded by William F. Buckley, which came out against him. During his campaign whole cross-sections of conservatives came out as 'Never Trump'.

To understand these fault lines it is worth remembering that after the cultural revolution of the 60s in the US, it wasn't the old-fashioned conservatives (whose entire way of being was seen as hopelessly square and un-modern) who really succeeded in taking on the cultural left but the much more intellectually equipped and rhetorically gifted neoconservatives. *Partisan Review* magazine, also a project of the anti-communist Cold War left soft-power CCF initiative, published an essay by Norman Podhoretz about the 'the know-nothing bohemians'. In it, he described 'the beat generation's worship of primitivism and spontaneity' that suggested a desire to 'kill those incomprehensible characters who are capable of getting seriously involved with a woman, a job, a cause.'

As Hartman elucidates in his book, many of the early neocons were New York Jewish intellectuals who had come to politics in the 30s through the City College of New York. These were smart, often working-class Jewish students who started out as Trotskyists and learned their style of debate in CCNY cafeteria's Alcove No. 1, where they argued with the Moscow-loyal communist students who occupied Alcove No. 2. During their later rightward turn, they worked on magazines *Commentary* and *Encounter*, the latter becoming the literary organ for the anti-Soviet soft-power CCF. This period produced writers and polemicists like Gertrude Himmelfarb and Irving Kristol.

Hartman also writes that even as they turned to the right they 'developed habits of mind that never atrophied' like their 'combative spirit, sweeping declarations and suspicion of leftist dogma. They maintained their Marxist style of diagnosing problems in relation to root causes, internal logics and overarching structures.' Having been Trotskyists themselves endowed them with an intuitive ability to critique the dogma of the left in a way that the churchgoing Christian conservative establishment couldn't. Similarly today, the troll-y version of the right that Milo represents is able to fight the new online identity politics in a way that actual conservatives are not able to. They understand the value of transgression, edginess and counterculture often better than their left-wing opponents.

What constitutes movements of the right and left in Anglophone culture wars discourse is based on a political compass that has long been reorienting, rethinking and reconstituting itself. In particular, class politics and social liberalism have not always sat comfortably together, nor did social conservatism with free -market economics for many decades until the neocons perfected the formula when in power. As Hartman reminds us, Christian figures like William Jennings Bryan merged concerns about the family with criticisms of capitalism, while before the 60s, American Prairie radicals organized under a populist banner against corporate monopolies and crony capitalism. Large numbers of workers joined trade unions in response to the Great Depression. Ideas of transgression and cultural radicalism were largely irrelevant to this working-class left. The 1962 Port Huron statement, the manifesto of the Students for a Democratic Society, contained a very different kind of message: 'We are people of this generation, bred in at least modest comfort, housed now in universities, looking uncomfortably at the world we inherit.' By the 1972 presidential campaign, the American Federation of Labor and Congress of Industrial Organizations abstained from supporting the Democratic candidate McGovern, because they saw him as a sell-out to identity politics. This was because of the party's adoption of 'New Politics', designed to bring identity groups to the forefront of politics while moving away from the centrality of economic inequality.

New Left thinker Herbert Marcuse meanwhile raised the question of 'whether it is possible to conceive of revolution when there is no vital need for it'. The need for revolution, he explained, 'is something quite different from a vital need for better working conditions, a better income, more liberty and so on, which can be satisfied within the existing order. Why should the overthrow of the existing order be of vital necessity for people who own, or can hope to own, good clothes, a well-stocked larder, a TV set, a car, a house and so on, all within the existing order?' In Marx's formulation, capitalism would lead to immiseration and so it was the urban industrial proletariat was was destined to be the revolutionary class. However, in the affluent society, according to Marcuse, the two great historical forces of the modern world, the bourgeoisie and the proletariat, 'no longer appear to be agents of historical transformation'. The working class had, according to many who shared this view, ceased being revolutionary and instead were becoming reactionary and culturally conservative, while the identity movements along race, gender and sexuality lines were becoming more radical than ever.

In academia, the 'cultural turn' saw a radical shift in scholarship whereby universities made culture the focus of contemporary debates. It also meant a shift in emphasis toward meaning and away from a positivist epistemology of discerning objective truth. Despite attempts to use the anti-postmodern language of real conservatives at times, Milo and his 4chan troll fans are in many ways the perfect postmodern offspring, where every statement is wrapped in layers of faux-irony, playfulness and multiple cultural nods and references.

Yiannopoulos's main enemy throughout his period of popularity in the US has been, above all else, feminism, so much so that he gained attention when he ran a quiz on Twitter asking his followers if they'd prefer to have (a) feminism or (b) cancer. Later, he adopted the slogan 'Feminism is cancer', which became available as a line of T-shirts. He regularly describes feminists as fat and his favorite choice of insult, 'lesbianic'. Here, he and Buchanan would find some common ground, but Buchanan and his fellow culture warriors believed that women's liberation and gay liberation were part of the same disease. This twin enemy loomed large in Buchanan's culture-wars speech as a measure of the moral decline of US society. Wrongly regarding Hillary

Clinton as a radical, as opposed to a thoroughly establishment baby boomer, he attacked her as well as Bill, saying:

> This, my friends, is radical feminism. The agenda that Clinton & Clinton would impose on America – abortion on demand, a litmus test for the Supreme Court, homosexual rights, discrimination against religious schools, women in combat units – that's change, all right. But it is not the kind of change America needs. It is not the kind of change America wants. And it is not the kind of change we can abide in a nation that we still call God's country.

When the Aids crisis hit, Buchanan wrote 'poor homosexuals... they have declared war upon nature and now nature is exacting an awful retribution.' The Stonewall riots of 1969 and the emergence of The Gay Liberation Front had profoundly changed sex in Western culture in ways that conservatives deeply regretted. Milo was part of a movement against overprotected students, but university campuses dropping their *in loco parentis* policies to protect the virginity of students was a major loss to the conservative establishment at the time. The acceptance of homosexuality had been part of a much broader freeing up of sexuality that both Milo and his Tumblr-dwelling gender fluid enemies continue to take influence from in different ways. *Time* magazine covered The Sexual Freedom League in 1966 and *The Joy of Sex* was published in 1972. Sexual revolution philosopher Norman O. Brown argued that by repressing our desire for 'polymorphous perversity' we had wrongly chosen the 'civilization' bargain in Freud's formulation.

Though Milo may seek to celebrate gay men and diminish feminism, gay and women's liberation have together loomed large in the conservative imagination as part of a declension narrative of Western civilization. The obsession with decline found on the alt-right today comes from a long conservative line of thought, who regularly drew upon books like Edward Gibbon's *The History of the Decline and Fall of the Roman Empire*, the eighteenth-century text that tied Rome's collapse to sexual decadence. Camille Paglia's work, greatly admired by Milo, is preoccupied with this same causal link between homosexuality, promiscuity, gender fluidity and civilizational decline. Neocon Gertrude Himmelfarb also used her scholarship of Victorian Britain to suggest that Western civilization had weathered the storm of modernity only because of its Victorian values, which had collapsed in the 60s owing to gay liberation and the sexual revolution.

In Yiannopoulos's speeches he made regular reference to partying and drinking, sometimes joking about drug-taking. He can barely go a few sentences without mentioning his homosexuality, anal sex jokes, and what sounds like a multitude of black sexual partners and boyfriends. Joking with Ann Coulter on his podcast, he said that he liked the idea of getting caught in bed with black drug-dealer boyfriends when he was rebelling against his parents. In one of his campus talks he dressed up as a camped up S&M cop to antagonize Black Lives Matter and had penis-shaped props.

In response to criticisms of his intentionally cruel bullying attacks on others, he simply shrugged them off as examples of fabulous catty gay male behavior. 4chan is also more of a product of the sexual revolution than of conservatism. From the start it was teeming with weird hardcore pornographic images and discussions – gay, straight, transgender and everything in between – and a culture of relish transgressing any and all moral codes when it comes to sexuality.

After the Islamist massacre in a gay nightclub in Orlando, Florida in 2016, Yiannopoulos traveled there to address a mourning crowd. He not only chose the moment to make the case against Muslim immigration, but also in favor of gun ownership – a very US-centric and perhaps conveniently acquired issue of little concern to British conservatives. The pro-gun cause would of course have enormous appeal to the right, but Yiannopoulos was also channeling a radical precedent like the black call to arms 'Negroes With Guns' by Robert F. Williams, which influenced the Black Panthers and other black self-defense militants.

On his podcast he also said that going to mass was the most 'punk' thing to do and that gays being accepted as part of mainstream society was 'boring'. In the online and on-campus culture war that Yiannopoulos fought, gays were no longer considered the harbingers of civilizational decline, while the finger of blame continued to be pointed at feminism and multiculturalism. Instead, he positioned gays as the saviors of civilization using many of the right's own ideas. On his campus tour he argued that gays are genetically destined to be the high-achieving protectors of Western civilization against feminism and Islam. Many conservatives who opposed gay liberation for decades suddenly embraced Milo's camp outrageousness in the name of kicking back against a common enemy by any means necessary. But in the end, when he had served his purpose in attracting to young rebels to the right, his outrageous sexual comments and camp demeanor proved too much of a liability.

Unlike Milo and his followers, Buchanan was also a supporter of censorship, especially for pornography, and in his culture-wars speech he said: 'we stand with President Bush in favor of the right of small towns and communities to control the raw sewage of pornography that so terribly pollutes our popular culture.' It's hard to imagine anything farther from the free-speech absolutism, the potty-mouthed black anal sex jokes, and the defense of rudeness against the 'pearl clutchers' of Yiannopoulos's camp persona and his cosmopolitan multicultural background.

He has acknowledged this distinction, saying:

The alt-right for me is primarily a cultural reaction to the nannying and language policing and authoritarianism of the progressive left—the stranglehold that it has on culture. It is primarily—like Trump is and like I am—a reaction against the progressive left doing today what the religious right was doing in the 90s—which is trying to police what can be thought and said, how opinions can be expressed.

In the culture wars Yiannopoulos invokes, Buchanan and the right *were* the chief anti-free speech pearl clutchers. Meanwhile, Andrea Dworkin and Catharine MacKinnon led the charge for censorship of pornography from the feminist side. Part of the success of the backlash against feminism in the 80s and 90s was as a result of the coalition with the historically doomed moral conservatives on their joint challenge to rising sexual libertinism in Western culture. On his show *The Firing Line*, William F. Buckley agreed with Andrea Dworkin on banning pornography. If one imagines where Milo would line up politically in terms of the infamous William F. Buckley v Gore Vidal televised presidential debates of 1968, it would probably be closer to that of Vidal, whose libertinism and mischievous gay rhetorical style was so abhorrent to Buckley.

The alt-right have described their movement as a reaction against establishment US conservatism, saying that there is a 'deep continuity' between the Buckleyite movement and the neocons. Spencer has also said, 'The left is the right and the alt-right is the new left' and that 'We're the ones thinking the impossible. We're the ones thinking the unthinkable.' On *Radix Journal* they draw on the idea of the 'The Fourth Political Theory', with reference to the Russian theorist Aleksandr Dugin and the French New Right's Alain de Benoist, an entirely new political ideology that integrates and supersedes liberal democracy, Marxism and fascism. Right-wing voices that claim to have been purged from the conservative movement, like Peter Brimelow and John Derbyshire, have formed part of the alt-right. It primarily opposes establishment political conservatism, as Kevin DeAnna explained in his influential essay for the alt-right, 'The Impossibility of Conservatism'.

The alt-right also seeks to destroy more than it proposes to build, unlike the institution-building and tradition-preserving ethos of the Burkean conservative movement, and seeks to smash some of the most treasured parts of US conservatism in particular, namely US exceptionalism – the notion dating back to Alexis de Tocqueville's *Democracy In America* of the US's unique founding on an idea rather than a blood and soil national identity. Vox Day's 'America is not an idea' or articles like 'Ideas didn't build America' in *The Right Stuff*, or VDARE's 'the "proposition nation" myth' all hammer this point.

In the end, Buchanan was one of the paleocons to back Trump and many of those who formerly loathed most of what Yiannopoulos and what he represented decided to change their minds and back the winning horse, not only of Trump, but also of the new libertines of the online irreverent 'punk' right. Having lost Buchanan's conservative culture war, they were perhaps strategically right to calculate that the only way they can ever have at least some of their ideas heard again would be to back a groping, lecherous, godless presidential candidate and a libertine figure such as Yiannopoulos and his army of online racist, foul-mouthed, porn-loving nihilists, who in many ways represent everything people like Buchanan are supposed to stand against. The rise of Milo, Trump and the alt-right are not evidence of the return of the conservatism, but instead of the absolute hegemony of the culture of non-conformism, self-expression, transgression and irreverence for its own sake – an aesthetic that suits those who believe in nothing but the liberation of the individual and the id, whether they're on the left or the right. The principle-free idea of counterculture did not go away; it has just become the style of the new right.

## Chapter Five

# From Tumblr to the campus wars: creating scarcity in an online economy of virtue

There are many potential explanations for the emergence of a new right sensibility among a younger generation, which rapidly shifted the range of acceptable discourse further to the right than anyone could have imagined. One is that long before it bubbled up to the surface of college campuses, and even Twitter and YouTube, it developed, in opposition to its enemy online culture of the new identity politics typified by platforms like Tumblr. They tried to move the culture in the opposite direction by restricting speech on the right but expanding the Overton window on the left when it came to issues of race and gender, making increasingly anti-male, anti-white, anti-straight, anti-cis rhetoric normal on the cultural left. The liberal online culture typified by Tumblr was equally successful in pushing fringe ideas into the mainstream. It was ultra-sensitive in contrast to the shocking irreverence of chan culture, but equally subcultural and radical.

In the aftermath of the Trump election, divisions within the broad 'left' became more prominent than ever. In particular, the animosity and deeper philosophical differences between the liberal left and the materialist left played out in insults being flung in both directions. Embittered that Hillary lost or that 'Bernie would have won' the socialists were labeled 'brocialists' and dismissed as arrogant 'white dudes', and in retaliation they hit back at preachy, performatively 'woke' Tumblr-style identity politics that they felt had destroyed the left. As well as brocialists and Berniebros, this milieu was even labeled 'alt-left'.

An account of this schism within 'the left', and an attempt to capture the online left identity politics culture that was every bit as influential, diffuse, multiplatform and constantly shifting as its rival culture on the right, is worth sketching out here.

Mainstream newsreading audiences were baffled when Facebook revealed it was offering over 50 gender options for its members to choose from in 2014 and around the same time the campus wars over safe spaces, trigger warnings, no-platforming and gender pronouns emerged. But the social media corporation was merely taking its cue from online subcultures that had been emerging for years before, and the youth political subcultures that had created them and emerged out of them. The main preoccupation of this new culture (the right named them SJWs and snowflakes, let's call it Tumblr-liberalism) was gender fluidity and providing a safe space to explore other concerns like mental ill-health, physical disability, race, cultural identity and 'intersectionality' – the now standard academic term for recognition of multiple varieties of intersecting marginalizations and oppressions. While the roots of this whole political sensibility may be found in academia and activist culture, its emergence into the mainstream that led to Hillary using terms like 'check your privilege' and 'intersectionality' was the culmination of years of online development on Tumblr, in fan cultures, on previous platforms like LiveJournal and on a mixture of social media.

Although one could trace various threads to a multitude of different online and offline points of origin, Tumblr was one of the most important platforms for the emergence of a whole political and aesthetic sensibility, developing its own vocabulary and style – very much the reverse mirror image of rightist 4chan in this way. It was here that what Walter Benn Michaels criticized as a liberal preference for 'recognition of diversity over economic inequality' reached its most absurd apotheosis with a politics based on the minutia and gradations of rapidly proliferating identities, and the emotional injuries of systemic cultural prejudices. Symbolic representative diversity and recognition became its goals, as it admonished transgressors for 'erasing my identity' and urged white/straight/male/cis people to 'listen' and 'believe'. If the generation of college-going millennials that followed the rise of this online culture could be described, as they are today by the conservative press in particular, as 'generation snowflake', Tumblr was their vanguard.

'One is not born, but rather becomes, a woman,' wrote French feminist and philosopher Simone de Beauvoir in 1949. By 1990, Judith Butler had taken this several steps further, or perhaps more literally, in *Gender Trouble: Feminism and the subversion of identity*, in which she argued that the coherence of the categories of sex, gender and sexuality were entirely culturally constructed through the repetition of styled and cultivated bodily acts, which created the appearance of an essential ontological 'core' gender.

By the early 2010s, Tumblr had put Butler's theory into practice and created an entire subcultural language, set of slogans and style to go with it. The most marked preoccupation of Tumblr's cultural politics has been identity fluidity, typically but not exclusively around gender. It was the subcultural digital expression of the fruition of Judith Butler's ideas. For years, the microblogging site filled up with stories of young people explaining and discussing the entirely socially constructed nature of gender and potentially limitless choice of genders that an individual can identify as or move between.

The following are just a few of the ever-expanding list of genders, now in the hundreds, all taken directly from Tumblr:

Alexigender – Gender identity that is fluid between more than one gender, but the individual cannot tell what those genders are.

Ambigender – A feeling of two genders simultaneously, but without fluidity/shifting. May be used synonymously in some cases with bigender.

Anxiegender – A gender affected by anxiety.

Cadensgender – A gender that is easily influenced by music.

Cassflux – When your level of indifference towards your gender fluctuates.

Daimogender – A gender closely related to demons and the supernatural.

Expecgender – A gender that changes depending on who you are around.

Faegender – A gender that changes with the seasons, equinoxes and moon phases.

Fissgender – A gender experience that is in some way split, similar to bigender or demigenders.

Genderale – A gender that is hard to describe. Mainly associated with plants, herbs and liquids.

Kingender – A gender somehow related to being otherkin.

Levigender – A lightweight, superficial gender you don't feel very much.

Necrogender – A gender that used to exist but is now 'dead' or nonexistent.

Omnigay – Genderfluid, with one's attraction to other genders changing with one's gender, so that the individual is always attracted to the same gender.

Perigender – Identifying with a gender, but not as that gender.

Polygenderflux – Having more than one gender, which intensity fluctuates.

Technogender – Only comfortable with one's gender when using technology/online, usually because of social anxiety (specialized for people with anxiety disorders).

Xoy – Someone who identifies in some way as a nonbinary boy or nonbinary boy-adjacent.

Xirl – Someone who identifies in some way as a nonbinary girl or nonbinary girl-adjacent.

These gender orientations on Tumblr are closely related to, and often make direct reference to, another online subculture of identity fluidity known as otherkin. This is a subculture of people who identify, according to the Wikipedia definition, as 'partially or entirely non-human' as mythical creatures, creatures from fantasy or popular culture including 'angels, demons, dragons, elves, fairies, sprites, aliens and cartoon characters'. Some claim to be able to 'astrally shapeshift', meaning that they experience the sense of being one of these creatures while not actually changing physically. Of course, as with all online culture, many Tumblr users use references to otherkin in a self-aware manner, almost as more of a knowing self-referential performance of belonging to a geeky subculture, but it does tell us something, as an extreme example, of the broader theme of identity fluidity that seems to run through it.

While gender non-conformism is nothing new, and has certainly been ever more mainstream since the beginning of the sexual revolution and the gay liberation movement, this is part of the creation of an online quasi-political culture that has had a huge and unexpected level of influence. Other similar niche online subcultures in this milieu, which were always given by the emerging online right as evidence of Western decline, also include adults who identify as babies and able-bodied people who identify as disabled people to such an extent that they seek medical assistance in blinding, amputating or otherwise injuring themselves to become the disabled person they identify as. You may question the motivations of the right's fixation on these relatively niche subcultures, but the liberal fixation on relatively niche sections of the new online right that emerged from small online subcultures is similar in scale – that is, the influence of Tumblr on shaping strange new political sensibilities is probably equally important to what emerged from rightist chan culture.

Professor Adolph Reed Jr. has often said liberals don't believe in actual politics anymore, just 'bearing witness to suffering'. The cult of suffering, weakness and vulnerability has become central to contemporary liberal identity politics, as it is enacted in spaces like Tumblr. It is also common in communities with a strong focus on gender fluidity to openly identify themselves as having disabilities and mental health issues that make them, by their own admission, extremely vulnerable and suffering. Some of the disabilities they describe can often be either psychological in origin or are unrecognized by modern medicine. One example of this is found in the 'spoonies' identity – an identification and online subculture in which members, typically young women, get spoon jewelry, spoon tattoos and put 'spoonie' in their social media biographies to signal their belonging.

'Spoonies' became known as such because of 'spoon theory'. The term was coined by Christine Miserandino in 2003 in her essay 'The Spoon Theory' (actually a metaphor), which was posted on her blog ButYouDon'tLookSick.com. She recalls a conversation in which a friend asked her what it was like to have an illness with no outwardly visible symptoms. Miserandino grabbed a handful of spoons from the table and and took them away one by one. Every spoon she then took away represented an event or activity of a typical day, demonstrating that her energy was very limited and, like everyone else's, finite. While caring about disabilities is something humans have been doing for centuries, and it's certainly uncontroversial, the online spoonie phenomenon became a subculture with a certain quasi-political zeal that seemed to characterize all the subcultures in the Tumblr identity-politics milieu. Young women, very often also identifying as intersectional feminists and radicals, displayed their spoonie identity and lashed out at anyone for not reacting appropriately to their under-recognized, undiagnosed or undiagnosable invisible illnesses or for lacking sensitivity to their other identities.

Self-flagellation also became a core characteristic of the new identity politics, especially among white, male, heterosexual, cis or able-bodied members of the subcultures, who were happy to 'check their privilege' – a phrase that became so central to Tumblr-liberal culture that is was often parodied by the right. As this privilege-checking culture made its way into mainstream discourse, anti-gamergate columnist Arthur Chu tweeted: 'As a dude who cares about feminism sometimes I want to join all men arm-in-arm & then run off a cliff and drag the whole gender into the sea.' On the morning following the election of Donald Trump, columnist Laurie Penny tweeted: 'I've had white liberal guilt before. Today is the first time I've actually been truly horrified and ashamed to be white.'

And yet, amid all the vulnerability and self-humbling, members of these subcultures often behaved with extraordinary viciousness and aggression, like their anonymous Pepe-posting counterparts, behind the safety of the keyboard. Jonathan Haidt's famous Atlantic essay in response to the mainstreaming of this sensibility on college campuses in the years that followed

'The Coddling of the American Mind' brought a discussion of 'generation snowflake' into mainstream discourse. But long before that obscure Internet spaces, subcultures and identifications fostered a culture of fragility and victimhood mixed with a vicious culture of group attacks, group shaming, and attempts to destroy the reputations and lives of others within their political milieu, later dubbed 'cry-bullying'.

While the right was developing its own critique of this strange world of online identity politics, an explosive essay by Marxist critic Mark Fisher appeared, called 'Exiting the Vampire Castle'. This inflamed the Tumblr-liberals and identitarian privilege-checking left further, and developed out into such vicious fights, call-outs and mass shamings, it ended up marking a split in left sensibilities for a younger generation that would grow in the years that followed between materialists of an older left style and those who adhere to this brand of pure identity politics. Fisher wrote:

'Left-wing' Twitter can often be a miserable, dispiriting zone. Earlier this year, there were some high-profile twitterstorms, in which particular left-identifying figures were 'called out' and condemned. What these figures had said was sometimes objectionable; but nevertheless, the way in which they were personally vilified and hounded left a horrible residue: the stench of bad conscience and witch-hunting moralism. The reason I didn't speak out on any of these incidents, I'm ashamed to say, was fear. The bullies were in another part of the playground. I didn't want to attract their attention to me.

And attract their attention he did. The deluge of personal and vindictive mass abuse experienced by Fisher for years afterwards, involving baseless accusations of misogyny, racism, transphobia, etc., became typical for anyone who dared to touch on any of the Tumblr left's key sensitivities, perhaps especially from a left perspective. The strangest feature of this online 'call-out culture' was this mixture of performative vulnerability, self-righteous wokeness and bullying. The online dynamics of this call-out culture were brilliantly described by Fisher as, 'driven by a priest's desire to excommunicate and condemn, an academic-pedant's desire to be the first to be seen to spot a mistake, and a hipster's desire to be one of the in-crowd.' I would add to this that the key driving force behind it is about creating scarcity in an environment in which virtue is the currency that can make or break the career or social success of an online user in this milieu, the counterforce of which was the anonymous underworld from which the right-wing trolling cultures emerged.

To give one of countless examples of this simultaneous victimhood and callousness, in 2016 it was reported in the news that an alligator snatched a 2-year-old boy at a Disney resort in Florida and dragged him into a lagoon. Despite the father's efforts to rescue him, the boy died – a devastatingly sad story to any normal mainstream audience. A Twitter user known on Twitter as 'Brienne of Snarth' with more than 11,000 followers and an influential Tumblr page criticized the grieving father of the toddler for his 'white privilege'. Evidence of her online life conformed to all the hallmarks of the Tumblr style of identity politics and like many of the loudest callers out of white privilege turned out to be white herself. She wrote: 'I'm so finished with this white privilege lately that I'm not even sad about a 2yo being eaten by a gator because his daddy ignored signs' and 'You really think there are no fucking consequences to anything. A goddam sign told you to stay out of the water in Florida. FUCK A SIGN.' Mainstream audiences were outraged when the consequent Twitter storm was reported, and the alt-right and alt-light were sharing it as evidence of the modern left's degeneracy, while in response many online Tumblr-liberals leaped to her defense.

In the early days of Twitter, a platform in which users are supposed to compete for followers and through which lagging careers can be instantly boosted through the correct virtue signaling, minor celebrities realized that one could attract a following greater than through traditional media. At first, self-righteously or snarkily denouncing others for racism, sexism or homophobia was the most instantaneous and certain way to achieve social media fame. Something about public social media platforms, it turned out, was conducive to the vanity of morally righteous politics and the irresistible draw of the culture wars. But soon the secret was out and everyone was doing it. The value of the currency of virtue that those who had made their social media cultural capital on was in danger of being suddenly devalued. As a result, I believe, a culture of purging had to take place, largely targeting those in competition for this precious currency. Thus, the attacks increasingly focused on other liberals and leftists often with seemingly pristine progressive credentials, instead of those who engaged in any actual racism, sexism or homophobia.

After the Orlando shooting, in which a man who pledged allegiance to Al Baghdadi had opened fire on a gay nightclub, millions rushed to Twitter, to publicly share their sadness and despair. In this moment of mass expression of pro-gay sentiment, this scarcity-creating purging process went into overdrive, to ensure that virtue could not be spread too thinly. One Twitter-famous intersectionalist admonished those who had called it the worst mass shooting in US history by reminding them that 'the worst was wounded knee'. Other similar tweeters raged against the use of the term Latina/o instead of Latinx in the reporting, while still others made sure to clarify that it was the shooter's mental illness, not his allegiance to ISIS and the caliphate, that caused the shooting. Not to be outdone, others then tweeted back angrily about the ableism of those who said the shooter had a mental illness. At one vigil to the atrocity where hundreds showed up, a young woman lashed out at the crowd: 'There are so many white people here. That wasn't a joke... Who are you really here for?'

These dynamics, which began in subcultural obscurity online, later spilled over into the campus wars over free speech, trigger warnings, the Western canon and safe spaces. Trigger warnings had to be issued in order to avoid the unexpectedly high number of young women who had never gone to war claiming to have post-traumatic stress disorder. They claimed to be 'triggered' by mention of anything distressing, a claim with no scientific basis and including everything from great works of classical literature to expressions of pretty mainstream non-liberal opinion, like the idea that there are only two genders.

At the height of all this Germaine Greer was announced to speak at Cardiff University about 'Women & Power: The Lessons of the 20th Century'. The women's officer at Cardiff University Students' Union, Rachael Melhuish, decided that Greer's presence would be 'harmful'. In her petition calling for the event's cancellation, she claimed:

> Greer has demonstrated time and time again her misogynistic views towards trans women, including continually misgendering trans women and denying the existence of transphobia altogether... Universities should prioritise the voices of the most vulnerable on their campuses, not invite speakers who seek to further marginalise them. We urge Cardiff University to cancel this event.

The petition was signed by over 2,000 people and Greer was transformed overnight from a leading veteran figure who worked for her entire life for the cause of women's liberation to a forbidden and toxic TERF (Trans-Exclusionary Radical Feminist), whose name was dragged through the dirt. As far as this new generation of campus feminists was concerned, Greer may as well have been on the far right. Greer had not published any comment about transgenderism for over 15 years, which

was 'not my issue', she later told *Newsnight*. In response to
the controversy, Cardiff University's vice-chancellor pandered
to those attacking Greer, saying: 'discriminatory comments of
any kind' and how it 'work(s) hard to provide a positive and
welcoming space for LGBT+ people'.

Not satisfied with the attacks on Greer thus far, online activist
Payton Quinn, identifying as 'non binary' and a 'trans feminist
activist and all round ethereal being' penned an angry public
letter suggesting Greer's actions were criminal in an article titled
'Entitled to Free Speech But Not Above the Law'.

In another previously unthinkable depth for the pro-
censorship left to plumb, Peter Tatchell, life-long veteran gay
activist who risked his life many times for the cause of gay
rights around the world, found himself at the center of the next
round of attacks. Fran Cowling, the student union's LGBTQI+
representative, said that she would not share a stage with a man
whom she regarded as having been racist, Islamophobic and
even 'transphobic'. Cowling refused an invitation to speak if
Tatchell attended. In the emails she cited Tatchell's signing of an
open letter in *The Observer* the previous year in support of free
speech and against campus no-platforming. When the debacle
gathered public attention afterwards, those on the anti-Tatchell
side doubled down, arguing that the resulting negative attention
they got amounted to harm and that he was being supported by
the right-wing press in his free-speech position, with some even
arguing he stage-managed the attacks against him.

In 2015, Iranian socialist and feminist Maryam Namazie was
invited to speak at Goldsmiths University, London. Because of
her militant secularism and open apostasy as an ex-Muslim, a
style that makes Western leftists uncomfortable, controversy
followed. The Islamic Society objected to her presence on campus
and when she spoke anyway, a gang of men from the society
sat in the front row of her talk trying to intimidate her. They
shouted over her, squared up to her, turned off her projector,

turned off the lights and for much of the talk she had to shout in order to be heard over them. Video evidence of the talk shows a level of intimidation that would be unthinkable if Namazie or her Islamist intimidators were white and western, and yet she not only didn't receive solidarity from her Western comrades, but she was also further condemned and attacked by them over the incident.

Goldsmiths Feminist Society came out in support of the Islamic Society against Namazie, and Goldsmiths LGBT Society released a statement in support of them also. To put in context those who the liberal students were defending at the expense of Namazie, the President of Goldsmiths Islamic Society, Muhammed Patel, was a supporter of hate-preacher Haitham al-Haddad, who in an article titled 'Standing up against Homosexuality and LGBTs' wrote, 'In order to combat the scourge of homosexuality Allah has ordained us to speak out, and that we should co-operate with others in righteousness and God-consciousness.'

Along with this series of attacks against these and other veteran figures of the new left, some on the right began to embrace being the target of such campaigns – a style Milo perfected. A noted difference, however, is that the right came out all guns blazing, while the left response was often to be baffled, cowed or apologetic and in some cases to retreat from the left itself. I often think the brain drain out of the left during this period because of the Tumblrization of left politics has done damage that will prove long-lasting.

In Canada Dr. Jordan Peterson became a hero of the alt-light after he refused to agree to legislation formalizing the use of alternative pronouns in his university, like 'ze' or 'zir' as alternatives to the old hat 'she' or 'he'. At an event to protest him, he appeared to speak to those who had gathered, and was drowned out by a white noise machine and was yelled at by members of the crowd. He also says the lock on his office door was glued shut, and his institution offered platitudinous support for his right to academic freedom and free speech, but warned he could get in legal trouble with the Ontario Human Rights code. The university received a wave of complaints from students and faculty that his criticisms of the new rules on pronouns were 'unacceptable, emotionally disturbing and painful'.

In March 2015, Laura Kipnis wrote an essay in *The Chronicle of Higher Education*, in which she criticized the atmosphere of 'sexual paranoia' on campuses, defended professor-student sexual relationships and criticized trigger warnings. A group of students protested in response, demanding that the administration reaffirm its commitment to the policies that Kipnis criticized. They carried a mattress—a reference to Emma Sulkowicz's earlier protest at Columbia University against rape on campus. Invoking university legislation, two grad students filed complaints against Kipnis, arguing that her article, which she has since expanded into a book, would deter students from reporting sexual misconduct. Kipnis publicly fought the attacks against her and was eventually exonerated.

These are just a few select cases in what felt like an endless stream of campus culture wars over these sexuality/gender/identity issues that emerged after years of a particular kind of identity politics being nurtured online. But how do these compare with past campus wars? William F. Buckley founded *National Review* as a 'counterestablishment' to the academic one and famously said: 'I'd rather entrust the government of the United States to the first 400 people listed in the Boston telephone directory than to the faculty of Harvard University.' In 1983 Robert Simonds, a spokesperson for the National Association of Christian Educators, said that a 'great war' was happening over education. Political commentator Walter Lippmann wrote: 'It is in the school that the child is drawn towards or drawn away from the religion and the patriotism of his parents.' And they were right to notice the 'long march through the institutions' that was taking place. Teachers in training were assigned books like

Friere's *Pedagogy of the Oppressed* and major culture-wars battles were waged over creeping feminism and multiculturalism in education and in the broader culture. Phyllis Schlafly's book *Child Abuse in the Classroom* on the same topic had a big influence on conservative mistrust of the liberal indoctrination at work in public schools.

At colleges and universities, debates about whether Stanford University should assign John Locke or Frantz Fanon played out, writes Hartman, and from the *Wall Street Journal* to books like *The Closing of the American Mind* by Allan Bloom, *Illiberal Education* by Dinesh D'Souza and *Tenured Radicals: How Politics Has Corrupted Our Higher Education* by Roger Kimball. Today, these same debates are playing out on college campuses with the 'decolonize our minds' movement and the campaign around 'Rhodes Must Fall' the successful attempt to pressure Cape Town University to have a statue of Cecil Rhodes removed. Members of the campaign later commented after they achieved their goal, 'the fall of "Rhodes" is symbolic for the inevitable fall of white supremacy and privilege at our campus.'

In 1988, students held a rally, chanting 'hey hey ho ho Western culture's got to go' over Standford's Western Civilization program, which sparked a huge culture war over the issue of a Western-centric canon. The pressure of the campaign resulted in the university's decision to modify the curriculum. Central to the undermining of the Western canon was the relativism of figures like literary theorist Stanley Fish, who undermined the idea of the stable meaning of texts and of a literary canon having objective timeless value: 'The only way we can hope to interpret a literary work is by knowing the vantage point from which we perform the act of interpretation.' Filled with like-minded academics, Duke University's English department became known as 'the Fish tank', that also promoted French theory in which universal claims about truth were represented as serving the interests of the powerful.

Camille Paglia later wrote: 'French theory is like those how-to tapes that guaranteed to make you a real estate millionaire overnight. Gain power by attacking power! Call this number in Paris now!' Bloom, also Paglia's Ph.D. supervisor, supported the idea of aesthetic and taste discrimination in the service of truth and beauty, and believed relativistic thinking was a slippery slope to nihilism. He wrote: 'Stanford students are to be indoctrinated with ephemeral ideologies and taught that there can be no intellectual resistance to one's own time and its passions'... 'This total surrender to the present and abandonment of the quest for standards with which to judge it are the very definition of the closing of the American mind and I could not hope for more stunning confirmation of my thesis.' This critique of liberal presentism has since been neatly summed up in the alt-right's use of the expression 'the current year' – a mocking way to describe the liberal insistence that 'you can't still hold that opinion, it's 2017!'

Todd Gitlin, a key figure in the Berkeley New Left movement, emerged as an internal critic of the left over that round of campus wars, arguing that the left 'marched on the English department while the right took the White House.' He believed that demands for equality should be grounded in universalism and believed academic relativistic notions of identity, which have today reached their logical conclusion in the Tumblr world of proliferating identities, represented the 'twilight of equality'. Also in parallel with the fallout from the online culture wars and contemporary campus and identity wars, Gitlin's critique of identity politics emerged when SDS was destroyed through internal divisions over universal goals and identity politics. He argued that the relativism of radicals would bring about the 'twilight of common dreams' arguing that: 'The cant of identity underlies identity politics which proposes to deduce a position, a tradition, a deep truth, or a way of life from a fact of birth, physiognomy, national origin, sex or physical disability.' In what could have come straight out of the mouth of Jordan Peterson or many others to his right today, Gitlin said 'a bitter intolerance emanates from much of the academic left.'

In 1996, a famous hoax that still haunts academe was perpetrated by Alan Sokal, a physics professor at New York University and University College London. He submitted an article to *Social Text*, an academic journal of postmodern cultural studies, whose editorial collective included stars at the time like Fredric Jameson and Andrew Ross, called 'Transgressing the Boundaries: Towards a Transformative Hermeneutics of Quantum Gravity'. It was intentionally 'liberally salted with nonsense' and proposed that gravity was a social construct. Sokal then revealed that the article was 'a pastiche of left-wing cant, fawning references, grandiose quotations, and outright nonsense.'

Today, this struggle over campuses continues, from Milo's tour to the Twitter account Real Peer Review, which publishes the titles and abstracts, sometimes with funny quotes, of absurd academic papers typically from cultural studies or theory-based journals, on everything from feminist analysis of glaciers to fat masculinities. Interestingly also to the contemporary context, after the Sokal affair an academic conference was called, with Judith Butler as a leading speaker, to deal with the emergence of something dubbed 'left conservatism'. This included figures like Sokal, who identified as on the left, and his left-wing supporters, including Barbara Ehrenreich, an idiosyncratic and independent-minded leftist who has always tended to write accessibly about issues of poverty and working-class life in books like *Nickle and Dimed*. The term 'conservative' here was of course meant pejoratively to expel certain people and thoughts – and those that might have been privately sympathetic to them – from respectable academic discourse.

Today, we are still having much the same culture war. If one had to pick a single thinker whose ideas have most shaped the

Tumblr left, it would undoubtedly be Judith Butler and those on the left who remain critics of that identity-oriented cultural left are still the kind of people who would align more closely with Gitlin and Ehrenreich. Paglia is now regarded as 'based goddess' by the alt-light and her work has been brought to a younger generation through Christina Hoff Sommers. The genuinely conservative right of Schlafly, meanwhile, is the only force described here that really has died, as the new right is as transgressive and rule-breaking as the new left once was. And yet on some of these issues like opposition to feminism, the canon, Cultural Marxism, the West and so on, the alt-right do carry their torch.

## Chapter Six

# Entering the manosphere

While feminism has expanded and thrived online in recent years so, too, has anti-feminist masculinist politics, which again developed in the context of evermore radical liberal gender politics and increasingly common anti-male rhetoric that went from obscure feminist online spaces to the mainstream. The 'red pill' metaphor that has been central to alt-right rhetoric has also been central to these anti-feminist masculinist political subcultures that constantly cross-pollinate with different layers of the online right. The many sites, subcultures and identifications associated with this anti-feminist online movement have grown and multiplied, to an extent that would undoubtedly have been written up as a 'digital revolution' if it had different cultural politics. These subcultures, between which there is often animosity, and some important political and philosophical difference, have become collectively referred to by some observers as 'the Manosphere'. The term has been used to describe everything from progressive men's issues activists dealing with real neglect of male health, suicide and unequal social services to the nastier corners of the Internet, filled with involuntary celibacy-obsessed, hate-filled, resentment-fueled cultures of quite chilling levels of misogyny.

Before delving into yet another aspect of the culture wars that typically generates all heat and no light, I'm not at all unsympathetic to the genuinely egalitarian goals of fairness also found in the men's rights movement. Fair and equal treatment in the courts should be a right to all people and the creeping underachievement of boys at school, the high suicide rates and the general culture of speaking about men with contempt all deserve criticism and need to be reformed. They are correct to argue that many feminists, a movement to which I belong, have often been intolerant and dogmatic on these issues. And yet, observing these online spaces, it is simply impossible to deny the rampant hateful misogyny, bitterness, conspiratorial thinking and generally foul character that seems to run through them. So it is worth saying first that my descriptions here are, like my descriptions of the worst of Tumblr-liberalism, 4chan and others, not representative of what you might call 'the men's movement' in general but of the darker online underbelly that has flourished online.

This crop of forum dwelling-obsessives would be horrified to learn that the original men's movement grew out of and alongside the feminist movement and the sexual liberation movement as a critique of rigid traditional sex roles, according to masculinities scholar Michael Kimmel. Men's liberation later grew apart from the feminist movement as second-wave feminism became increasingly antagonistic towards men, criticizing men as a whole in its rhetoric around rape and domestic violence. Splits and tendencies developed as the question of men's experience of their societal role took different thinkers and factions in radically different directions. It was by the 90s that the men's movement became primarily focused on institutions in which men were excluded or discriminated against.

Different types of men's movements existed across this trajectory. In the UK there were progressive groups like Men Against Sexism and the New Men's Movement, which would both be labelled 'manginas' by today's charming brand of alt-right tinged online anti-feminists. Under the banner of the 'men's movement' in the US there have been groups with diverse orientations from Christian men's groups like the Promise Keepers to the mythopoetic movement of the poet Robert Bly, which searched for a male authenticity lost by life in a modern, feminized, atomized society. It was in the 90s, during what journalist Susan Faludi described as a 'backlash' against second-wave feminism, in the US in particular, that the formulation of the men's movement that we associate with the term today gained prominence, which necessitated a certain antagonism toward feminism.

The critique of the restrictive traditional male sex role gave way to a celebration of masculinity itself, while feminism became the political enemy force. This wave of more overtly anti-feminist men's politics included the National Coalition of Free Men, who took influence from books like Warren Farrell's *The Myth of Male Power* and Neil Lyndon's *No More Sex War: The Failures of Feminism*. They rejected the idea of male privilege and focused on discrimination against fathers and violence against men. But even the most militantly anti-feminist forms of pre-Internet men's rights activism now seem supremely reasonable and mild compared with the anti-feminism that emerged online in the 2010s. A more openly hateful culture was unleashed under the conditions of anonymity and it took on a more right-wing character, living up to the most negative feminist caricatures of men's rights activism – rage-filled, hateful and chauvinistic.

The Reddit subforum The Red Pill has been central to the online development and resurgence of this anti-feminist politics online. At the same time as these anti-feminists were using the term to describe their awakening from the blissful mind prison of liberalism into the unplugged reality of societal misandry, the hard alt-right was embracing the term to describe their equivalent racial awakening. On AlternativeRight.com 'the red pill' and 'being red pilled' was one of the central metaphors and favorite expressions. On Reddit's Red Pill forum, men discussed false rape accusations, female-on-male violence, cultural misandry, avoidance of 'pedestalling pussy' and 'game' – meaning a style of 'pick up artist' dating advice that began with Neil Strauss's 2005 book *The Game*. Looking back today, Strauss's book seems pretty mild and inoffensive, certainly compared to today's online pickup artistry forums, which tend to read like a sinister Darwinian guide to tricking the loathed female prey into surrender. Discussions on these issues on various Reddit forums and other forums within the anti-feminist manosphere are a pretty relentless flow of sexual frustration, anxiety about evolutionary rank and foaming-at-the-mouth misogyny full of descriptions of women as 'worthless cunts', 'attention whores', 'riding the cock carousel', and so on.

One of the dominant and consistent preoccupations running through the forum culture of the manosphere is the idea of beta and alpha males. They discuss how women prefer alpha males and either cynically use or completely ignore beta males, by which they mean low-ranking males in the stark and vicious social hierarchy through which they interpret all human interaction. Some follow the pickup artistry of bloggers like Roosh V in order to rise from a 'nice guy' beta to a sexually successful alpha. Roosh (aka Daryush Valizadeh) began as a pickup artist, later self-described as a neo-masculinist and flirted with the hard alt-right, who he would have found common ground with in their shared belief that feminism is a major cause of civilizational decline. He positively reviewed alt-right writer Kevin MacDonald's *The Culture of Critiques* and titled it, 'The Damaging Effects Of Jewish Intellectualism And Activism On Western Culture'.

He became known first, however, for a series of books called Bang, which advocate the aforementioned style of aggressive, manipulative, social-Darwinist-tinged approach to coaxing women to have sex, in which he travels to different countries taking notes on strategy and then advises his followers. Always the romantic, he used the ebooks and blogs to detail the 'ruthlessly optimized process' that 'enabled me to put my penis inside' various women. His website, called Return of Kings, is one of the more notorious of the misogynist sites in the manosphere.

Roosh V doesn't identify with equality-based men's rights activism or the MGTOW movement, calling them 'sexual losers' and 'bitter virgins'. Return of Kings has included titles such as 'Biology Says People on Welfare Should Die', 'Don't Work for a Female Boss' and '5 Reasons to Date a Girl With an Eating Disorder'. He has said he would not perform oral sex on a woman for quasi-political reasons. He complained about women in Denmark, and claimed that because of the strong welfare state and feminist culture, he didn't have much sexual success with them on his Bang tour. Interviewed from a mystery location in Eastern Europe, he said he preferred it there because the women were more 'traditional'.

He also saw Trump's win as a victory for his movement, saying: 'I'm in a state of exuberance that we now have a President who rates women on a 1–10 scale in the same way that we do and evaluates women by their appearance and feminine attitude,' adding 'We may have to institute a new feature called "Would Trump bang?" to signify the importance of feminine beauty ideals that cultivate effort and class above sloth and vulgarity.'

Roosh V attracted attention internationally for a blog post that he wrote titled 'How to Stop Rape' in which he said:

If rape becomes legal under my proposal, a girl will protect her body in the same manner that she protects her purse and smartphone. If rape becomes legal, a girl will not enter an impaired state of mind where she can't resist being dragged off to a bedroom with a man who she is unsure of—she'll scream, yell, or kick at his attempt while bystanders are still around. If rape becomes legal, she will never be unchaperoned with a man she doesn't want to sleep with. After several months of advertising this law throughout the land, rape would be virtually eliminated on the first day it is applied.

He claims that the piece was 'satire'. How it would work as satire remains unclear, but it is not altogether implausible that it was some kind of attempt at a satirical or knowing tone that just didn't quite work. It didn't work primarily because his own views are too close to those being described satirically, so there is no level of knowing absurdity to them. A typical example of his style would be quotes like: 'My default opinion of any girl I meet is worthless dirty whore until proven otherwise.' Let's just say it was not quite Swift. As a result of the piece, a petition was launched on Change.org that called for Roosh V to be banned from Canada, which gathered over 38,000 signatures.

Closer to an older style of men's rights politics, as distinct from the PUA or cultural politics of Reddit, the website A Voice for Men is perhaps the most important men's rights movement website around right now, and it was founded and run by Paul Elam. To give a sense of the tone of the site, on the main page at the time of writing they're advertising two books. The first is called *Memoirs of a Misogynist: An Erotic Novel for Men*, and the second is called *The Seduction of Anita Sarkeesian* and features a scraggily drawn cartoon of Anita with her hand down her pants on the cover accompanied with the description '... if you hate Anita, then why not irritate her by purchasing a copy?' Featured articles include '13 reasons women lie about rape' and 'All women are pedophiles and that's all they are' – a reference to Marilyn French's 'All men are rapists and that's all they are' from 1978. The site often reads like a catalog of the very worst rhetorical excesses in the history of feminism but with the sexes reversed.

In 2011, Elam established the vigilante doxxing site Register-Her.com, which publishes the personal information of women the site claims 'have caused significant harm to innocent individuals either by the direct action of crimes like rape, assault, child molestation and murder, or by the false accusation of crimes against others.' This vigilante strategy became widespread on both sides of the culture wars and will always entail serious real-world consequences like harassment and stalking, the loss of reputation, work and relationships. While the list included women who have been sent to prison for various crimes, it also included others who were acquitted and listed female rape victims whose court cases didn't result in a full conviction as a 'false accuser'.

In an unflattering Buzzfeed profile, Elam's ex-wife and daughter say he abandoned his wife and children twice, from two separate families, and they say he has only been able to make A Voice for Men his full-time job because of the women who have financially supported him throughout his life. He has compared the family court system's treatment of fathers to Jim Crow saying 'fathers are forced to pay child support like it was mafia protection money', and accused his first wife of lying about rape in order to relinquish his own parental rights to avoid paying child support, according to the profile. Despite having had a violent and abusive father, Elam claims he realized at a young age that it was a 'woman's world'.

He used to blog under the name 'The Happy Misogynist'. In 2011, feminist writer Jessica Valenti's personal information was added to Register Her and Elam said on radio, 'We're gonna be all over her like Ron Jeremy on a drug-addled bimbo.' Valenti claims she was so overwhelmed with threatening abuse that she contacted the FBI and left her house until things died down. In one post, he wrote:

All the PC demands to get huffy and point out how nothing justifies or excuses rape won't change the fact that there are a lot of women who get pummeled and pumped because they are stupid (and often arrogant) enough to walk [through] life with the equivalent of a I'M A STUPID, CONNIVING BITCH – PLEASE RAPE ME neon sign glowing above their empty little narcissistic heads.

To an outsider there may seem to be total coherence within the anti-feminist Internet, but it is actually wracked with as much infighting as you find among any political subculture. A few important sites in the manosphere throughout the online culture wars, some now defunct or banned, included Reddit's PhilosophyOfRape, in which you could find topics like the promotion of 'corrective rape' against feminists, The Counter-Feminist, Love-shy.com, /r/mensrights, The Anti-Feminist, SlutHate.com and /r/incel for the involuntarily celibate beta male. Advice seeking in anti-feminist and pickup artist (PUA) forums often comes from self-identifying 'nice guys', whose commentary on women suggests their sense of self may be a little lacking in honest reflection. There are also PUA-hate forums, for those who are critical of pickup artistry as a scam that places too much of the responsibility on men to change their own behavior through bodybuilding and learning 'game' just to impress 'stupid sluts', by which they simultaneously always seem to mean women who they're angry at because they *won't* put out.

In the more explicitly alt-right crossover sites, as the anti-feminist sphere and the race-oriented sphere started to meet, Chateau Heartiste is an MRA and PUA blog run by James C. Weidmann (aka 'Roissy in DC'), which mixes evolutionary psychology, anti-feminism and white advocacy. In the blog he argues that women's economic freedom is leading to civilizational collapse. He believes white civilization is being destroyed by miscegenation, immigration and low white female birth rates owing to feminism. This decline can only be undone, he thinks, by deporting minorities and restoring patriarchy.

Anti-feminist blogger Vox Day identifies with the alt-right and was an early supporter of gamergate. He is also the author of *SJWs Always Lie: Taking Down the Thought Police*. Like all of the anti-feminist alt-right, he also believes that feminism in the West is a civilizational threat. He opposes the concept rape within marriage, for example, saying: 'The concept of marital rape is not merely an oxymoron, it is an attack on the institution of marriage, on the concept of objective law, and indeed, on the core foundation of human civilization itself.' Jack Donovan is another significant MRA alt-right crossover, as a self-proclaimed 'androphile' who has written for AlternativeRight.com.

The Men Going Their Own Way (MGTOW) movement is a straight male separatist group whose members have chosen (ahem) to avoid romantic relationships with women in protest against a culture destroyed by feminism, and to focus instead on individual achievement and independence from women. The rhetoric suggests punishment and revenge are at the heart of their motivations, as their advice is usually peppered with references to a 'bitch' who will cheat, leave, use you for your money and so on. They like to discuss women 'riding the cock carousel' throughout their twenties, and then entering their thirties and finding that their 'stocks' on the dating scene have started to fall. Like the alt-right they believe feminism has destroyed Western civilization, etc., etc., and that women will either trick them into raising children that aren't theirs, get pregnant intentionally in order to trap them, or falsely accuse them of rape.

In just about any YouTube video that touches on men's issues you'll find MGTOW adherents in the comment thread depicting women as worthless and mindlessly led by biological impulses, and saying that marriage should be boycotted. There are four levels of MGTOW, and adherents often signal their stages of progression and the amount of time they've *'been mig-tow'*. Level 0 is where the member 'takes the red pill' and rejects feminism. At level 1 MGTOWs reject long-term relationships, at level 2 they reject short-term relationships and hook-ups, level 3 requires economic disengagement from women and level 4 is societal disengagement, where the man refuses to interact with an entire society poisoned by feminism. In their forums they discuss one-night stands, while others rely solely on masturbation or prostitution, depending on their level.

An article by Milo in *Breitbart* on 'the Sexodus' helped make

MGTOW famous. In it, he wrote encouragingly about men's flight from women, romance, sex and marriage as a consequence of pervasive feminism – something he seems to change his mind about, sometimes arguing feminism is ubiquitous, sometimes arguing it's deeply unpopular with women because of its misandry. MGTOW are not to be conflated with other militantly anti-feminist movements, however. An article on Return of Kings called 'Virgins Going Their Own Way' described MGTOW as 'The creeping cult of male loserdom', resulting in much internal squabbling within the anti-feminist Internet. In the many YouTube videos devoted to MGTOW, usually under a pseudonym and with no images of the speaker, a strangely common feature is a kind of robotic voice, almost like a newsreader, an unconvincing voice of ultra-rationality to conceal what seems like a great deal of bitterness and hurt at rejection.

The most amusing of all these is the Proud Boys movement, who have a kind of Fred Perry-wearing, skinhead punk aesthetic and want to spread the 'No Wanks' doctrine. Its founder is Gavin McInnes and their tenets include, according to him, 'minimal government, maximum freedom, anti-political correctness, anti-racial guilt, pro-gun rights, anti-Drug War, closed borders, anti-masturbation, venerating entrepreneurs, venerating housewives.' McInnes has compared it to the hardcore scene in the 80s, 'where there wasn't really a boss'.

The scene produces its logos, tattoos and imagery in a punk-inspired leaderless DIY way. It also has a quasi-ironic frat-style system of hazing and again a system of 'levels'. First level Proud Boy simply requires declaring yourself a Proud Boy. To ascend to a second level Proud Boy you must adhere to 'No Wanks' (they use the hashtag #NoWanks), meaning you limit pornography and masturbation to once a month, and you also have to get a beating until you can name five breakfast cereals. The third level involves getting a tattoo declaring your allegiance to Proud Boys and No Wanks. Masturbation and pornography are central to the (like *Vice*, sort of tongue-in-cheek but sort of not) Proud Boys philosophy. McInnes has said, 'Gen X guys, it's making you weaker and stupider and lazier. And millennials, well, it's making you not even want to pursue relationships.' He encourages young men to instead 'throw down bricks', which means to approach women in real life. The thinking behind Proud Boys features some of the general declension narratives shared by the alt-right and the conservative tradition, in particular Western decline and decadence owing to the rise of liberalism and feminism: 'With all liberal concepts, we wiped out tradition and replaced it with something worse.'

A frustrating contradiction and hypocrisy you find in many of these online spaces and subcultures is that they want the benefits of tradition without its necessary restraints and duties. They simultaneously want the best of the sexual revolution (sexual success with pornified women, perpetually dolled up, waxed and willing to do anything) without the attendant insecurities of a society in which women have sexual choice and freedom. So, for example, Roosh V complains about the low morals of 'sluts', but writes an entire series called Bang about random promiscuous sex with women, strangers he seems to actively dislike. In the case of Proud Boys, as ridiculous as you feel even saying the name, there is an attempt at some certain internal coherence to its moral system. Proud Boys seeks to return to a more traditional way of life, but it also adopts a conservative approach to pornography and masturbation, and claims to 'honor the housewife'. It's still not much of a recommendation, but perhaps it is less overtly hateful towards women at least in principle.

And yet McInnes was the ultimate partying hipster hedonist, largely responsible for the whole *Vice* magazine style. His show features female porn star guests and he rates women out of ten. This glaring contradiction runs through all of the alt-right when it comes to women. The most important space for the production of alt-right and alt-light aesthetics for years has been 4chan, which is full of pornography that is so disturbing and so intentionally dehumanizing that anyone other than a moral and emotional derelict would be repulsed by it instead of chuckling idiotically, as they seem to do.

Lastly, and most interestingly, F. Roger Devlin is an alt-right writer, a white nationalist, an MRA and anti-feminist, read by MGTOW adherents and a range of rightist anti-feminists. He is perhaps one of those who has attempted to theorize a more serious anti-feminist politics. Devlin is a contributing editor to *The Occidental Quarterly: Western Perspectives on Man, Politics and Culture* and also writes for VDARE. His essay 'Sexual Utopia in Power' argues against 'today's sexual dystopia, with its loose morals and confused sexual roles.' It explores 'female hypergamy (mating up), narcissism, infidelity, deceptiveness, and masochism.' It also argues that 'the breakdown of monogamy results in promiscuity for the few, loneliness for the majority.'

On this last point, I think he's getting to the central issue driving this kind of reactionary sexual politics, perhaps even the central personal motivation behind the entire turn to the far right among young men. The sexual revolution that started the decline of lifelong marriage has produced great freedom from the shackles of loveless marriage and selfless duty to the family for both men and women. But this ever-extended adolescence has also brought with it the rise of adult childlessness and a steep sexual hierarchy. Sexual patterns that have emerged as a result of the decline of monogamy have seen a greater level of sexual choice for an elite of men and a growing celibacy among a large male population at the bottom of the pecking order. Their own anxiety and anger about their low-ranking status in this hierarchy is precisely what has produced their hard-line rhetoric about asserting hierarchy in the world politically when it comes to women and non-whites. The pain of relentless rejection has festered in these forums and allowed them to be the masters of the cruel natural hierarchies that bring them so much humiliation.

This psychological compensation is nothing new. Nietzsche's fetish for physical male strength, hierarchy and the exertion of will, which his Nazi followers were attracted to in his writing, contrasted in a similarly pathetic way to the reality of his physical state – myopia, nervous prostration, chronic ill-health, digestive disorders and of course the bitter rejection by women.

Celibate and romantically rejected young men fill spaces like Reddit's incel subforum for the involuntarily celibate, where they go to seek advice and express their sexual frustration. At the time of writing, the latest post on the /r/incel reads: 'I spent 4 hours just staring at the wall in my room. What normies call an existential crisis, for the incel is simply... life.' It has been from this celibate milieu that the racial hierarchical politics of the alt-right has drawn, not exclusively, of course, but its recurrence as a theme is telling. These frustrated young men are first exposed to social-Darwinian thinking about attracting a mate in the name of 'game', then to the misogynist rhetoric about women's evil narcissistic nature when the gaming doesn't work. Look at the comment section of any of the vast and ever-growing genres of anti-feminist YouTube videos and you'll quickly find rhetoric about women being worthless, sluts, stupid, fat, lazy, shallow, hysterical, untrustworthy and justly deserving of violent retribution. Because of the level of cross-pollination between the manosphere and the alt-right, it would be impossible at this point for them not to be exposed to those ideas eventually. Certainly, their anger at their low-ranking position in the sexual pecking order can occasionally burst forth in extreme ways.

One of those who took the violent fantasies of these forums into real life was the 'virgin killer' Elliot Rodger, who drove to a University of California–Santa Barbara sorority house with a plan to massacre the women inside. When he couldn't gain entry to the building, Rodger shot at random people outside, in the end killing mostly men. The rampage ended when police found him dead in his car with a gunshot wound to the head. Rodger had uploaded a final video to YouTube, titled 'Elliot Rodger's Retribution'. In it, he described his desire to punish women for rejecting him:

> Well, this is my last video, it all has to come to this. Tomorrow is the day of retribution, the day in which I will have my revenge against humanity, against all of you... I've been through college for two and a half years, more than that actually, and I'm still a virgin. It has been very torturous... I don't know why you girls aren't attracted to me, but I will punish you all for it... I'm the perfect guy and yet you throw yourselves at these obnoxious men instead of me, the supreme gentleman.

The term 'supreme gentleman' has remained a joke on the anti-feminist Internet ever since and Rodger has become a comical archetypal figure of the angry beta male. Rodger also left behind a lengthy autobiographical manuscript, titled *My Twisted World*. He described his sexual frustration, his hatred of women who kept thwarting his desire to have sexual relationships with them, his bitter loathing of those sexually successful men, who he also called 'brutes' and 'animals', and his contempt for interracial couples in which a white woman coupled off with a man Rodger saw as genetically inferior to him. He mentions a 'War on Women':

> The Second Phase will take place on the Day of Retribution itself, just before the climactic massacre... My War on Women... I will attack the very girls who represent everything I hate in the female gender: The hottest sorority of UCSB.

On 4chan the day the story broke, one contributor posted an image of Rodger and wrote: 'Elliot Rodger, the supreme gentleman, was part of /b/. Discuss.' Commenters replied: 'That dude was fairly good looking. He must've just been the beta to end all betas if he never got laid.' Another wrote: 'Manifesto had "I do not forget, I do not forgive" and "kissless virgin", etc., he was a /b/tard.' Rodger's 'I do not forget, I do not forgive'.

After the killing, one reporter was contacted by a fellow online community member of PUAhate on Reddit, an incel forum used regularly by Rodger, who explained that the community was wrongly 'being depicted as a place where bitter men sat around discussing their hatred of women.' In a typical type of response one is always faced with when trying to describe how jaw-droppingly hate-filled these spaces can be, the journalist was assured that the forum was 'more light-hearted than violent'. He also noted that the forum user's chosen pseudonym right after the killing spree was 'ElliotRodgerIsAGod'.

# Chapter Seven

# Basic bitches, normies and the lamestream

In the aftermath of Trump's election, one of the more sympathetic types of analysis found everywhere from *The Guardian* to the *Financial Times* framed Trump's victory as one that reflected the views of 'ordinary people' who felt 'left behind'. Thomas Frank was one of the most insistent voices from the left articulating this critique of disdainful liberal elitism, saying:

> We cannot admit that we liberals bear some of the blame for its emergence, for the frustration of the working-class millions, for their blighted cities and their downward spiraling lives. So much easier to scold them for their twisted racist souls, to close our eyes to the obvious reality of which Trumpism is just a crude and ugly expression: that neoliberalism has well and truly failed.

Although the idea that ordinary people felt alienated by political correctness was not uncommon in right-wing rhetoric, there was also quite a remarkable shift from a subcultural elitism to a sudden proletarian righteousness, or even a bit of *noblesse oblige*, as though the right had been making Thomas Frank's argument all along. In reality they had been making pro-inequality, misanthropic, economically elitist arguments for natural hierarchy all along. As I noted previously in a 2017 piece for *The Baffler*, Ann Coulter had long drawn upon the elite fear of the hysterical and easily led crowd. In her book *Demonic: How the Liberal Mob is Endangering America* explaining how 'the liberal mob is destroying America' she drew upon Gustave LeBon, the misanthropists' favorite theorist of the masses. Her writing on overbreeding, overcrowding swarms of immigrants is a direct continuation of this theme, which has been consistent in elite circles since the beginning of industrialized urbanized mass society, first applied to their multiplying native proletariat and later to new waves of immigrants.

Before the 'ordinary people' narrative became suddenly ubiquitous on the new online right after the election results, Milo could be seen in photo shoots wearing a 'Stop Being Poor' T-shirt, a quote from the heiress Paris Hilton, one of his idols. After the election results he was giving talks about the white working class. The hard alt-right had also rejected the idea that the masses were their naturally traditionalist allies any longer, as the conservative establishment had typically believed. Instead, they had argued that the great mass of society had been tainted and indoctrinated by liberal feminist multiculturalism, and were close to beyond redemption. It was no longer 'five minutes to midnight' as the anti-immigration right had long claimed but well past midnight. While the Trumpians are busy quickly rewriting history, it is important to remember that behind the 'populist' president, the rhetoric of his young online far-right vanguard had long been characterized by an extreme subcultural snobbishness toward the masses and mass culture.

American writer David Auerbach explained that one of the defining features of what he called A-culture, or anonymous chan culture, was 'the constant hazing of n00bs through argot and complex conventions and elite technical knowledge polices the boundaries of the subculture to inoculate it from massification.' Gabriella Coleman wrote that 'trolling proliferated and exploded at the moment the Internet became populated with non-technologically-minded people' and went on to say 'Trolls work to remind the masses that have lapped onto the shores of the Internet that there is a class of geek who, as their name suggests, will cause Internet grief, hell, misery.' Although Coleman's description contains more than a hint of admiration and subtle nod of approval, to me this goes to the very heart of how vile and misanthropic the whole culture around the chans is and has always been, not in spite of but because of its countercultural style and sensibility. That it eventually fused so completely with the alt-right makes perfect sense.

Swastika-tattooed Nazi hacker and troll weev, who Coleman has always written flatteringly about, elaborated his views on the masses in an interview:

> Trolling is basically Internet eugenics. I want everyone off the Internet. Bloggers are filth. They need to be destroyed. Blogging gives the illusion of participation of a bunch of retards... We need to put these people in the oven... We are headed for a Malthusian crisis. Plankton levels are dropping. Bees are dying. There are tortilla riots in Mexico, the highest wheat prices in 30-odd years... The question we have to answer is: How do we kill four of the world's six billion people in the most just way possible?

This misanthropy and anxiety over the breeding of lower orders is one of the most dominant features of alt-right discourse from the foul-mouthed chaos of chan culture to the more serious long-form theory of the alt-right proper. But this is nothing new. Literary critic John Carey wrote about Malthusian, eugenicist and other elite prejudices against emerging mass society and mass culture. During the nineteenth century, he explains, the poorer section of Europe's population *tripled*, and industrialization crammed more and more workers into previously elite urban cultural spaces. H. G. Wells despaired at the 'extravagant swarm of new births' and called it 'the essential disaster of the twentieth century', a sentiment echoed by weev nearly a hundred years later. What Yeats called the 'spread of democratic vulgarity' and mass literacy was quickly changing the nature of the divide between the elite and the rapidly expanding masses.

This discourse seems to be channeled today by the new

online far right but through a subcultural anti-mainstream style, which has been more palatable to academia and to progressives because they recognize this countercultural elitism from their own political circles. We can see some kind of hybrid of these sensibilities in the online spaces from which rightist trolling styles and much of the current anti-feminism is generated – a mix of the Nietzschean misanthropic sensibility and the more counterculture-tinged *Fight Club* referencing one. Nietzsche, by far the most influential thinker across all of the strands that make up the alt-right, warned that 'a declaration of war on the masses by higher men is needed' to dominate 'the superfluous'.

Early on, the reaction of mainstream conservative media to Internet trolls from the chan world was an unambiguously moral and condemnatory one, and the standard progressive academic reflex (implicitly pro-counterculture, implicitly pro-transgression) was less critical, verging on celebratory. The Fox News depiction of 4chan as an 'Internet hate machine' and trolls more broadly as an anti-social, foul-mouthed group of misanthropes, still living with their mothers, etc., simultaneously mocked and heightened the moral panic about the anarchy of the online world.

Other mainstream news media focused on cyberbullying, DDoS attacks and the trolling of Facebook memorial pages. Author Whitney Phillips was more ambivalent, characterizing the cultural politics of trolling in more generous terms than the mainstream press, portioning some of the blame for their extreme cruelty to Facebook policies and the 'encoded solipsism' of the social network itself. While she recognized the very real impact of their actions on their victims, Philips described 4chan/b/'s trolls as 'revel[ing] in counter-hegemony' and 'undermining established media narratives' and the 'mindless histrionics of the modern 24-hour news cycle'. She characterized Fox News' unflattering description of 4chan trolls as an attempt to 'maximize audience antipathy' toward them and said 'mainstream media outlets aim to neutralize a particularly counter-hegemonic cultural space.'

As late as 2014, when 4chan was full of extreme racist and misogynist content, Gabriella Coleman wrote in much more positive tones again about the hacker cultures that had emerged from it:

> What began as a network of trolls has become, for the most part, a force for good in the world. The emergence of Anonymous from one of the seediest places on the Internet is a tale of wonder, of hope, and of playful illusions. Is it really possible that these ideals of collectivity and group identification, forged as they were in the hellish, terrifying fires of trolling, could transcend such an originary condition? Did the cesspool of 4chan really crystallize into one of the most politically active, morally fascinating, and subversively salient activist groups operating today? Somewhat surprisingly, yes.

Years before the whole 4chan troll culture became a central force behind the entire aesthetics and humor of the alt-right, it was teeming with racism, misogyny, dehumanization, disturbing pornography and nihilism. Even taking into account the complex and shifting nature of chan culture, it is certainly hard to imagine even a hint of approval being tolerated in academia if the subjects at hand were ordinary blue-collar members of the far right like Tommy Robinson, despite his far milder views than what has characterized 4chan and trolls like weev for many years. It was the utterly empty and fraudulent ideas of countercultural transgression that created the void into which anything can now flow as long as it is contemptuous of mainstream values and tastes. This is what allowed a culture that has now been exposed in all its horror to be romanticized by progressives as a counter-hegemonic force. The truth I think it reveals is that both rightist chan culture and ultra-PC academic culture understood the countercultural dog whistle of disdain for anything mainstream.

In a 2016 essay 'The New Man of 4chan', I wrote an account of the racist and misogynist incel mass shooter Chris Harper Mercer, whose killing spree killed nine and injured nine. In response to a 4chan thread believed to have been started by him, describing a killing that the author was going to commit, a commenter wrote: 'Make sure you got molotovs. It is really easy and painfully [sic] way to kill many normies.' Another wrote that 'Chads and Stacy's' should be targeted, referencing a 4chan meme about the normies. Chad Thundercock and his female equivalent, Stacey, are embodiments of this normies meme.

I would argue there is a much more critical way of theorizing these online cultures and it comes from the study of music subcultures. Chad and Stacey bring to mind the more feminine but similarly frowned upon 'Sharon and Tracey' in cultural critic Sarah Thornton's study of 'subcultural capital' in pop subcultures and countercultures. In her book about club cultures, she wrote:

> If girls opt out of the game of hipness they will often defend their tastes with expression like 'it's crap but I like it'. In doing so they acknowledge the subcultural hierarchy and accept their lowly position within it. If, on the other hand they refuse this defeatism female clubbers and ravers are usually careful to distance themselves from the degraded pop culture of 'Sharon and Tracey'; they emphatically reject and denigrate a feminized mainstream.

She criticized what was known as the Birmingham School in subcultural studies, which produced analysis of subcultures often as radical, transgessive and counter-hegemonic. She argued that this orthodoxy had 'been insufficiently critical of subcultural ideologies, first, because they were diverted by the task of puncturing and contesting dominant ideologies and second because *their biases have tended to agree with the anti-mass society discourses of the youth cultures they study.*' [emphasis mine]. While even critics of the alt-right and rightist chan culture have found themselves trying to use and 'get' its slang and niche subcultural references and in-jokes, Thornton applied sociologist Pierre Bourdieu's concept of *cultural capital* in her theory of *subcultural capital* as the central motivating factor at work in the club cultures of the 90s. Elite subcultural knowledge or hipness, she argued, was a form of cultural capital, through which members of the subculture gain entry. Bourdieu, from whom her term was adapted, argued that 'the deep-seated intention of slang vocabulary is above all the assertion of an aristocratic distinction.'

While cultural capital was once earned through being urbane and well-mannered, subcultural capital is earned, Thornton argued, through being 'in the know', using obscure slang and using the particularities of the subculture to differentiate yourself from mainstream culture and mass society. Thornton argues that the media plays a key role in the system, through which the subculture gives meaning to what is in or out of fashion, high or low in subcultural capital. Like many online cultures, club culture, she argues, polices the boundaries of its subcultures through constant reclassification of hipness.

The hatred of the shallow, vain, clueless girl with mainstream tastes trying to infiltrate a geeky subculture has become central to geeky subcultures. A common trope employed across a variety of geek alt-right subcultures is that of the girl who is trying to belong to geek subcultures, but who fails to use the correct markers of belonging, such as correct slang and depth of elite knowledge.

The entire discourse around 'normies' and 'basic bitches' who 'don't get' the countercultural styles of the amoral subculture takes me back to my adolescent days of rival music subcultures, but now it's with grown men and some more serious political stuff at stake. Richard Spencer regularly accuses those who fail to find the return of race separatism edgy and cool of being normies and basic bitches. Mike Cernovich was interviewed by the *New York Times* and said Hillary Clinton's speech 'was the stupidest thing she could have done', adding, 'Her social-media advisers are twenty-four-year-old basic bitches who feel triggered by us...' When we've reached a point where the idea of being edgy/countercultural/transgressive can place fascists in a position of moral superiority to regular people, we may seriously want to rethink the value of these stale and outworn countercultural ideals.

One can also hear echoes of Nietzsche in some of the attacks on increasingly feminized mainstream online platforms. Music critic Robin James wrote that: 'Nietzsche's ascription of feminine characteristics to the masses is always tied to his aesthetic vision of the artist-philosopher-hero, the suffering loner who stands in irreconcilable opposition to modern democracy and its inauthentic culture.' And John Carey claimed: 'Nietzsche's view of the mass was shared or prefigured by most of the founders of Modern European culture.' The online expression 'there are no girls on the Internet' appeared early on in 4chan's 'Rules of the Internet'. This is intended to be read not literally but as an assertion that the areas of the Internet in which there are few or no women constitutes 'the Internet', meaning the authentic Internet. Women are discussed in a way that presumes their absence, and users seemed to treat the anonymous space as a place where grievances could be aired against women to a sympathetic implicitly male audience.

'Cumdumpster', a slang term that was popular on the anti-feminist Internet for many years, has its roots in attacks against women perceived to be attention-seeking and vain, moving into male-dominated geeky spaces. As scholar Vyshali Manivannan documented, the common usage of the term on 4chan originates in 2008 in an infamous incident in which a 4channer identifying as a 'femanon' posted a photo of what looked like herself in lingerie, almost certainly fake. The woman requested advice on a recent breakup, asking whether or not she could easily commit marital infidelity. Her behavior was in such breach of subcultural conventions that users began editing the post, according to Manivannan, expressing her interest in excrement and exchanging the word femanon for cumdumpster. The thread was temporarily fixed to the front page of /b/ and one user deemed it the equivalent to 'a human head on a pike', a clear statement of inclusion and exclusion.

Although it had since become less influential, one geeky online subculture that started to move to the right and shared many characteristics of the contemporary alt-right was 'new atheism'. It was one of the predecessors to the alt-light, with an underlying Christopher Hitchens style of hitting out at the irrational and the faithful. All the 'Milo OWNS stupid feminist' type of videos today are made with much the same style as the new atheist videos that were equally numerous on YouTube a few years before with titles like 'HITCHSLAP. Hitchens OWNS stupid Christian woman'. It also had the same Nietzschean, anti-mainstream, non-conformist sensibility running through it.

Female 'new atheist' Rebecca Watson was the founder of the Skepchick blog and also cohosted The Skeptics' Guide to the Universe podcast. Back in 2011, Watson became the object of a wave of abuse in the online atheist and skeptic community at the center of an online storm now known as #elevatorgate. She had written a blog titled 'Reddit makes me hate atheists' about incidents of young women in the atheist online community being ridiculed for trying to engage in discussion in the largely male forums. In June of 2011, she was speaking on a panel with Richard Dawkins. According to her account of the event that led to #elevatorgate:

I used my time to talk about what it's like for me to communicate atheism online, and how being a woman might affect the response I receive, as in rape threats and other sexual comments. The audience was receptive, and afterward I spent many hours in the hotel bar discussing issues of gender, objectification, and misogyny with other thoughtful atheists. At around 4 a.m., I excused myself, announcing that I was exhausted and heading to bed in preparation for another day of talks. As I got to the elevator, a man who I had not yet spoken with directly broke away from the group and joined me. As the doors closed, he said to me, 'Don't take this the wrong way, but I find you very interesting. Would you like to come back to my hotel room for coffee?' I politely declined and got off the elevator when it hit my floor.

She referred to this incident in a vlog afterwards. As a result, the comment sections on her YouTube videos were flooded with nasty sexualized abuse and threats, her Wikipedia page was vandalized and, she wrote: 'A few individuals sent me hundreds of messages, promising to never leave me alone.' The hate mail was further intensified after Richard Dawkins himself weighed in, mocking Western feminists for complaining about such trivial things as being propositioned in an elevator, when much greater suffering was taking place in the Muslim world.

Twitter accounts were made in her name and used to tweet incriminating things to her friends and others. Entire blogs were created about her, she claimed, cataloguing past mistakes and attempting to dig up anything incriminating in her past. Just a week after Dawkins weighing in, she was scheduled to speak at an atheist conference, and a man tweeted Watson that he was attending and that if he ran into her in an elevator, he'd assault her.

Hated for destroying a male space with their feminine culture, other women and feminists in the atheist online community have reported similar behavior. Watson's co-blogger, Amy Davis Roth, had to move house after her address was posted on a forum dedicated to hating feminist atheists, called Slime

Pit. These had been posted by the same man who had written a scathing post about her on A Voice For Men. Feminist skeptic blogger Greta Christina wrote that: 'when I open my mouth to talk about anything more controversial than Pan Galactic Gargle Blaster recipes or Six More Atheists Who Are Totally Awesome, I can expect a barrage of hatred, abuse, humiliation, death threats, rape threats, and more.' Similarly, skeptic Jennifer McCreight stopped blogging and accepting speaking engagements altogether, writing: 'I wake up every morning to abusive comments, tweets, and emails about how I'm a slut, prude, ugly, fat, feminazi, retard, bitch, and cunt (just to name a few)... I just can't take it anymore.'

A meme said to have originated from Reddit, in the atheist forum r/atheism, to show how women use photo-based social media to indulge their vanity while men do not, showed a cartoon of a male forum user showing their audience a brick, which appears as simply a brick, while the female forum user showing the audience a brick appears in a posed and flattering photo of her holding a brick. In this cartoon image, the female is more interested in taking a photo of herself under the pretence of displaying an interest in the object under discussion, while the male simply displays the object.

This image featured in the r/atheism forum, documented by feminists critical of the culture of online atheism, when a 15-year old girl under the pseudonym Lunam, posted a thread called 'What My Super Religious Mother Got Me For Christmas', in which she linked to a photo of herself holding Carl Sagan's *Demon-haunted World: Science as a Candle in the Dark*. The first comment on the image read, 'Brace yourself, the compliments are coming', suggesting the inevitability of the flattery she would knowingly receive. What followed was a long discussion, in which commenters discussed her age, and joked about abducting and anally raping her. 'Relax your anus, it hurts less that way' wrote one commenter. 'Blood is mother nature's lubricant' joked another. When Lunam eventually responded to these comments, she wrote: 'Dat feel when you know you'll never be taken seriously in the atheist/scientific/whatever community because you're a girl' and the first critical response returned 'well if you say things like "dat feel"...'

This was part of a broader trend within male-dominated geeky online subcultures whereby women are viewed as a threat to the edginess of the subculture, instead seen as a force for bringing the moral and behavioral constraints and the inauthenticity of the mainstream platforms into the subcultural realm. An early example of the anti-female geek genre, the 'Idiot Nerd Girl' meme, which appeared around May 2010, featured a photo of a teenage girl wearing thick-rimmed glasses with the word 'nerd' written on the palm of her hand. The upper caption contained references to 'geek culture', while the bottom caption demonstrates a lack of subcultural knowledge, captioned with things like: 'Self-proclaimed title of "Nerd"/What is World of Warcraft?' or 'I love back to the future!/What the hell is a gigawatt?'

Women who find themselves called attention-seeking whores, camwhores and cumdumspters with regularity in forums that identify as transgressive and countercultural are usually guilty of slipping up and 'not getting' the subcultural conventions. They are seen to display female vanity, which is violently rejected in chan culture because it is the defining feature of so much of mainstream social media and online culture, in which networks such as Instagram and Facebook are based around personal identity and photographs. It is against these massified and feminized networks that these subcultures aggressively seek to defend their borders.

Again, this is nothing new. In reference to John Osbourne's *Look Back in Anger* and *Rebel Without a Cause*, as a similarly gendered attack on the mediocrity of the post-war social order, Joy Press and Simon Reynolds wrote: 'The rebel discourse of the 50s is haunted by the figure of the matriarch as the chief organiser of conformism.' In *One Flew Over the Cuckoos's Nest* the rebellious inmate Harding warns against the evil nurse Ratched: 'We are victims of the matriarchy here my friends.' Conformity in this imaginary is feminine and rebellion is masculine.

Misanthropy and misogyny, hatred of the breeding domesticating feminine, going together in the world of the alt-right is also nothing new. In *The Sex Revolts* Reynolds and Press argued that, in the rebel imagination, women figure as both victims and agents of 'castrating conformity'. This link is particularly evident in the concept of momism, in Philip Wylie's *Generation of Vipers* from 1942, a polemic on the degeneration of US society, engulfed by materialism and shallow feminized popular and consumer culture. As in the anti-feminist 'red pill' online cultures, the trap of marriage and domesticity was posited as the enemy in 50s and 60s male rebel culture, and women regularly played the roles of the counter-revolutionary enforcers of suburban mediocrity.

The negative association of femininity and mass culture goes back further again. Literary critic Andreas Huyssen traces it back to *Madame Bovary*. Written at a time in which the fathers of Modernism expressed 'an aesthetic based on the uncompromising repudiation of what Emma Bovary loved to read', the novel presented an unflattering portrait of a woman addled by romantic fiction. Huyssen saw the *Other* of this period as woman. In the era of the first major women's movement, he argued, the enemies at the gate of a male-dominated elite were female:

It is indeed striking to observe how the political, psychological, and aesthetic discourse around the turn of the century consistently and obsessively genders mass culture and the masses as feminine, while high culture, whether traditional or modern, clearly remains the privileged realm of male activities.

I want to return again to *Fight Club*. 4chan's original set of 50 'Rules of the Internet', which listed 'tits or GTFO' and 'there are no girls on the Internet', also lists the first two rules as 'You do not talk about /b/' and 'You do NOT talk about /b/', mimicking the first two rules of *Fight Club*: 'You do not talk about *Fight Club*'.

Tyler Durden, the lead character from the movie, embodies the reassertion of rebel masculinity against the emasculating conformity of consumer culture and the post-industrial feminized timidity of white-collar office life. Edward Norton's character is the conformist, emasculated, consumerist beta male while his alter ego of sorts, Durden, is the countercultural alpha because he is free from needing or being controlled by women. The Pink Soap he sells is made from the reconstituted fat of women who had undergone liposuction and then had their fat 'sold back to them', which fuses rebellion against consumerism with a disdain for feminine vanity and crushing conformity – perhaps the central theme in MGTOW culture. It also constructs a rebel masculinity that rejects both traditional male roles and pro-feminist new ones as its anti-conformist antidote.

The rhetoric of so much of the alt-right echoes Durden's anti-conformist, anarchic style in the movie, in which he attempted to wake the conformist drone from his slumber, to red pill himself. Echoing the rebel masculinity of 60s counterculture and the ideas about masculinity found on the alt-right, Durden described mainstream masculinity as:

> … slaves with white collars. Advertising has us chasing cars and clothes, working jobs we hate so we can buy shit we don't need. We're the middle children of history, man. No purpose or place. We have no Great War. No Great Depression. Our Great War's a spiritual war… our Great Depression is our lives. We've all been raised on television to believe that one day we'd all be millionaires, and movie gods, and rock stars.

But we won't. And we're slowly learning that fact. And we're very, very pissed off.

This has become precisely also the rhetorical tone and style of the MGTOW movement and the anti-feminist manosphere in general, in which the absent father is often the basis for further blaming women.

In *Fight Club,* the cuck theme is also there. The narrator, Jack, tells us 'like so many others I had become a slave to the IKEA nesting instinct' as he sits on the toilet looking at an IKEA catalog. Durden later asks him, 'Why do guys like you and I know what a duvet is?' Like the online right, it incorporates masculinist and anti-feminist politics, as well as rebel angst and a rejection of the domesticating, feminine influence of women. In the discursive style of the new 'punk' transgressive online right, nesting is also associated with pacification, while transgression, pornography and depictions of violence are employed as its counterforce in online hate campaigns against women who encroach upon their space.

The pop culture cliché of the *American High School* movie, which adapted old archetypes, depicted a social world in which the worst sexists were always the all brawn no brains sports jock. But now that the online world has given us a glimpse into the inner lives of others, one of the surprising revelations is that it is the nerdish self-identifying nice guy who could never get the girl who has been exposed as the much more hate-filled, racist, misogynist who is insanely jealous of the happiness of others. Similarly, the idea of the inherent value of aesthetic qualities that have dominated in Western pop culture since the 60s, like transgression, subversion and counterculture, have turned out to be the defining features of an online far right that finds itself full of old bigotries of the far right but liberated from any Christian moral constraints by its Nietzschean anti-moralism. It feels full of righteous contempt for anything mainstream, conformist, basic. Instead of pathetically trying to speak the language of this new right by trying to 'troll the trolls' or to mimic its online culture, we should take the opportunity to reject something much deeper that it is revealing to us. The alt-right often talk about the mind prison of liberalism and express their quest for that which is truly radical, transgressive and 'edgy'. Half a century after the Rolling Stones, after Siouxsie Sioux and Joy Division flirted with fascist aesthetics, after *Piss Christ*, after *Fight Club*, when everyone from the President's fanboys to McDonalds are flogging the dead horse of 'edginess', it may be time to lay the very recent and very modern aesthetic values of counterculture and the entire paradigm to rest and create something new.

## Conclusion

# That joke isn't funny anymore – the culture war goes offline

During the period examined in this book, Mark Fisher stood out as one of the few voices not on the right who had spoken out against the anti-intellectual, unhinged culture of group hysteria that gripped the cultural left in the years preceding the reactive rise of the new far right online. In January 2017, when news broke that Fisher had committed suicide, those in the same online milieu that had slandered and smeared him for years responded as you might expect—by gloating.

Stavvers (aka Another Angry Woman), an influential Twitter figure among what the alt-right call SJWs, had already written 'Vampires Castle' sarcastically down as her Twitter location and responded to the news of his death by tweeting: 'Just because Mark Fisher is dead, doesn't make him right about "sour-faced identitarians". If only left misogyny would die with him,' with the follow-up: '*dons vampire cape, flies off into the night*,' This response is a fairly typical example of precisely the sour-faced identitarians who undoubtedly drove so many young people to the right during these vicious culture wars. The left's best critic of this disease of the left had just died and dancing on his grave was a woman who once blogged about baking bread using her own vaginal yeast as a feminist act.

There is no question but that the embarrassing and toxic online politics represented by this version of the left, which has been so destructive and inhumane, has made the left a laughing stock for a whole new generation. Years of online hate campaigns, purges and smear campaigns against others – including and especially dissident or independent-minded leftists – has caused untold damage. This anti-free speech, anti-free thought, anti-intellectual online movement, which has substituted politics with neuroses, can't be separated from the real-life scenes millions saw online of college campuses, in which to be on the right was made something exciting, fun and courageous for the first time since... well, possibly ever. When Milo challenged his protesters to argue with him countless times on his tour, he knew that they not only wouldn't, but also that they couldn't. They come from an utterly intellectually shut-down world of Tumblr and trigger warnings, and the purging of dissent in which they have only learned to recite jargon.

The online right in return has become nastier still, with many drifting so far right it would have been inconceivable just a few short years ago, to Jewish conspiracies and so on. Wherever you find even the lightest version of the online right, in forums, in YouTube comments, on Twitter, you will now also find a deluge of the worst racial slurs imaginable, vicious commentary about women and ethnic minorities, and fantasies of violence against them. Inevitably, the Jewish conspiracies and dehumanizing invective against 'rapugees' also follows. Even conservatives are starting to catch a glimpse of the level of inhumanity that the culture wars have released on the right. When David French of the *National Review* dared to criticize Trump, for example, he first got attacked by Milo and then the alt-right attack dogs came. He wrote:

> There is nothing at all rewarding, enjoyable, or satisfying about seeing your beautiful young daughter called a 'niglet'. There is nothing at all rewarding, enjoyable, or satisfying about seeing man after man after man brag in graphic terms that he has slept with your wife. It's unsettling to have a phone call interrupted, watch images of murder flicker across your screen, and read threatening e-mails. It's sobering to take your teenage kids out to the farm to make sure they're both proficient with handguns in case an intruder comes

when they're home alone. The misery is compounded when longtime friends and allies dismiss my experiences and the experiences of my colleagues as nothing more than the normal cost of public advocacy. It's not. I have contributed to *National Review* for more than ten years now, and have been deeply involved in many of America's most emotional culture-war battles for more than 20. I've never experienced anything like this before.

Multiple journalists and citizens have described in horrifying detail the attacks and threats against those who criticize Trump or figures of the online Trumpian right, especially if the critic is female, black or Jewish, but also if they're a 'cuckservative'. They now have the ability to send thousands of the most obsessed, unhinged and angry people on the Internet after someone if they dare to speak against the president or his prominent alt-light and alt-right fans. Although the mainstream media is still quite anti-Trump, it would be naïve to think this isn't going to result in a chilling of critical thought and speech in the coming years, as fewer and fewer may have the stomach for it.

In February 2017, before the spectacular collapse of his career, Milo had planned to give the closing talk of his tour on the campus of UC Berkley, home of the free-speech movement of the left in 1964. Many have commented on the irony of the Berkeley riots that took place – the historical reversal of the left now censoring the campus to cleanse it of the right – but it is also significant that it was on what was scheduled to be the final night of his tour. It was on this night, at the end of a yearlong tour throughout which the US campus left spectacularly failed to challenge him on the level of ideas, that it chose to riot. Like the now famous Richard Spencer getting punched meme, it felt as though a giddy display of momentary muscle provided a temporary relief from the unfamiliar feeling of relentlessly losing.

Video footage quickly emerged on Twitter the night of the riot of a young female Yiannopoulos fan being maced in the face, another young woman being struck on the head with a flagpole and a man lying on the ground unconscious being beaten by several people while a voice off-camera screamed 'beat his ass!' The glass walls at the ground floor of the building were smashed, fires were started and Yiannopoulos was evacuated, canceling the talk. On this night the right was on the receiving end of violence, but on another, an anti-Milo protester was shot.

His tour painfully exposed the deep intellectual rot in contemporary cultural progressivism and it found itself completely unable to deal with the challenge coming from the right. The problem with the contemporary style of Tumblr-liberalism and a purely identitarian self-oriented progressivism that fomented in online subcultures and moved on to college campuses is that the very idea of winning people over through ideas now seems to anguish, offend and enrage this tragically stupefied shadow of the great movements of the left, like the one that began on campuses like Berkeley in 1964. Milo may be vanquished but not through a battle of ideas.

The online culture wars of recent years have become ugly beyond anything we could have possibly imagined and it doesn't look like there is any easy way out of the mess that has been created. Suddenly, how far away the utopian Internet-centric days of the leaderless digital revolution now seem, when progressives rejoiced that 'the disgust' had 'become a network' and burst suddenly into real life. Now, one is almost more inclined to hope that the online world can contain rather than further enable the festering undergrowth of dehumanizing reactionary online politics now edging closer to the mainstream but unthinkable in the public arena just a few short years ago.

Zero Books

# CULTURE, SOCIETY & POLITICS

Contemporary culture has eliminated the concept and public figure of the intellectual. A cretinous anti-intellectualism presides, cheer-led by hacks in the pay of multinational corporations who reassure their bored readers that there is no need to rouse themselves from their stupor. Zer0 Books knows that another kind of discourse – intellectual without being academic, popular without being populist – is not only possible: it is already flourishing. Zer0 is convinced that in the unthinking, blandly consensual culture in which we live, critical and engaged theoretical reflection is more important than ever before.

If you have enjoyed this book, why not tell other readers by posting a review on your preferred book site.

# Recent bestsellers from Zero Books are:

### In the Dust of This Planet
Horror of Philosophy vol. 1
Eugene Thacker
In the first of a series of three books on the Horror of
Philosophy, *In the Dust of This Planet* offers the genre of horror
as a way of thinking about the unthinkable.
Paperback: 978-1-84694-676-9 ebook: 978-1-78099-010-1

### Capitalist Realism
Is there no alternative?
Mark Fisher
An analysis of the ways in which capitalism has presented itself
as the only realistic political-economic system.
Paperback: 978-1-84694-317-1 ebook: 978-1-78099-734-6

### Rebel Rebel
Chris O'Leary
David Bowie: every single song. Everything you want to know,
everything you didn't know.
Paperback: 978-1-78099-244-0 ebook: 978-1-78099-713-1

### Cartographies of the Absolute
Alberto Toscano, Jeff Kinkle
An aesthetics of the economy for the twenty-first century.
Paperback: 978-1-78099-275-4 ebook: 978-1-78279-973-3

**Malign Velocities**
Accelerationism and Capitalism
Benjamin Noys
Long listed for the Bread and Roses Prize 2015, *Malign
Velocities* argues against the need for speed, tracking
acceleration as the symptom of the ongoing crises of capitalism.
Paperback: 978-1-78279-300-7 ebook: 978-1-78279-299-4

**Meat Market**
Female Flesh under Capitalism
Laurie Penny
A feminist dissection of women's bodies as the fleshy fulcrum
of capitalist cannibalism, whereby women are both consumers
and consumed.
Paperback: 978-1-84694-521-2 ebook: 978-1-84694-782-7

**Poor but Sexy**
Culture Clashes in Europe East and West
Agata Pyzik
How the East stayed East and the West stayed West.
Paperback: 978-1-78099-394-2 ebook: 978-1-78099-395-9

**Romeo and Juliet in Palestine**
Teaching Under Occupation
Tom Sperlinger
Life in the West Bank, the nature of pedagogy and the role of a
university under occupation.
Paperback: 978-1-78279-637-4 ebook: 978-1-78279-636-7

**Sweetening the Pill**
or How we Got Hooked on Hormonal Birth Control
Holly Grigg-Spall
Has contraception liberated or oppressed women? *Sweetening the Pill* breaks the silence on the dark side of hormonal contraception.
Paperback: 978-1-78099-607-3 ebook: 978-1-78099-608-0


**Why Are We The Good Guys?**
Reclaiming your Mind from the Delusions of Propaganda
David Cromwell
A provocative challenge to the standard ideology that Western power is a benevolent force in the world.
Paperback: 978-1-78099-365-2 ebook: 978-1-78099-366-9